DEPARTMENT OF THE TREASURY TECHNICAL EXPLANATION OF THE CONVENTION BETWEEN THE GOVERNMENT OF THE UNITED STATES OF AMERICA AND THE GOVERNMENT OF THE DEMOCRATIC SOCIALIST REPUBLIC OF SRI LANKA FOR THE AVOIDANCE OF DOUBLE TAXATION AND THE PREVENTION OF FISCAL EVASION WITH RESPECT TO TAXES ON INCOME SIGNED AT COLOMBO MARCH 14, 1985, AS AMENDED BY A PROTOCOL SIGNED AT WASHINGTON ON SEPTEMBER 20, 2002

DEPARTMENT OF THE TREASURY TECHNICAL EXPLANATION OF THE
CONVENTION BETWEEN THE GOVERNMENT OF THE UNITED STATES OF
AMERICA AND THE GOVERNMENT OF THE DEMOCRATIC SOCIALIST
REPUBLIC OF SRI LANKA FOR THE AVOIDANCE OF DOUBLE TAXATION
AND THE PREVENTION OF FISCAL EVASION WITH RESPECT TO TAXES ON
INCOME SIGNED AT COLOMBO MARCH 14, 1985, AS AMENDED BY
A PROTOCOL SIGNED AT WASHINGTON ON SEPTEMBER 20, 2002

This is a Technical Explanation of the Convention between the Government of the United States of America and the Government of the Democratic Socialist Republic of Sri Lanka for the Avoidance of Double Taxation and the Prevention of Fiscal Evasion with Respect to Taxes on Income Signed at Colombo March 14, 1985 (the "Convention"). The Convention was amended by a Protocol signed on September 20, 2002 (the "Protocol"), which was accompanied by an explanatory Exchange of Notes (the "Notes").

Negotiations with respect to the Protocol took into account the U.S. Treasury Department's current tax treaty policy and the U.S. Treasury Department's Model Income Tax Convention published September 20, 1996 (the "U.S. Model"). Negotiations also took into account the Model Income Tax Convention on Income and on Capital, published by the Organization for Economic Cooperation and Development (the "OECD Model"), the United Nations Model Double Taxation Convention Between Developed and Developing Countries (the "UN Model"), and recent tax treaties concluded by both countries.

The Technical Explanation is an official guide to the Convention. It reflects the policies behind particular Convention provisions, as well as understandings reached with respect to the application and interpretation of the Convention.

References in the Technical Explanation to "he" or "his" should be read to mean "he or she" and "his or her."

Article 1 (Personal Scope)

Paragraph 1

Paragraph 1 of Article 1 provides that the Convention applies to residents of the United States or Sri Lanka, except where the terms of the Convention provide otherwise. Under Article 4 (Resident) a person is generally treated as a resident of a Contracting State if that person is, under the laws of that State, liable to tax therein by reason of his domicile or other similar criteria. If, however, a person is considered a resident of both Contracting States, a single state of residence (or no state of residence) is assigned under Article 4. This determination generally governs for purposes of the Convention.

Certain provisions of the Convention are applicable to persons who may not be residents of either Contracting State. For example, Article 20 (Government Service) may apply to an employee of a Contracting State who is resident in neither State. Paragraph 1 of Article 25 (Nondiscrimination) applies to nationals of the Contracting States. Under Article 27 (Exchange of Information and Administrative Assistance), information may be exchanged with respect to residents of third states.

Paragraph 2

Paragraph 2 of Article 1 states the generally accepted relationship both between the Convention and domestic law and between the Convention and other agreements between the Contracting States (i.e., that no provision in the Convention may restrict any exclusion, exemption, deduction, credit or other allowance accorded by the tax laws of the Contracting States, or by any other agreement between the Contracting States). The relationship between the non-discrimination provisions of the Convention and other agreements is addressed not in paragraph 2, but in paragraph 5.

Under paragraph 2, for example, if a deduction would be allowed under the U.S. Internal Revenue Code ("the Code") in computing the taxable income of a resident of Sri Lanka, the deduction also is allowed to that person in computing income under the Convention. Paragraph 2 also means that the Convention may not increase the tax burden on residents of the Contracting States beyond the burden determined under domestic law. Thus, a right to tax given by the Convention cannot be exercised unless that right also exists under internal law.

It follows that under the principle of paragraph 2 a taxpayer's U.S. tax liability need not be determined under the Convention if the Code would produce a more favorable result. A taxpayer may not, however, choose among the provisions of the Code and the Convention in an inconsistent manner in order to minimize tax. For example, assume a resident of Sri Lanka has three separate businesses in the United States. One is a profitable permanent establishment and the other two are trades or businesses which would earn taxable income under the Code but which do not meet the permanent establishment threshold tests of the Convention. One of these trades or businesses is profitable and the other incurs a loss. Under the Convention, the income of the permanent establishment is taxable, and both the profit and loss of the other two businesses are ignored. Under the Code, all three would be subject to tax, but the loss would offset the profits of the two profitable ventures. The taxpayer may not invoke the Convention to exclude the profit of the profitable trade or business and invoke the Code to claim the loss of the losing trade or business against the profit of the permanent establishment. *See* Rev. Rul. 84-17, 1984-1 C.B. 308. If, however, the taxpayer invokes the Code for the taxation of all three ventures, the taxpayer would not be precluded from invoking the Convention, for example, with respect to any dividend income the taxpayer may receive from the United States that is not effectively connected with any of the taxpayer's business activities in the United States.

Nothing in the Convention can be used to deny any benefit granted by any other agreement between the United States and the other Contracting State. For example, if certain benefits are provided for military personnel or military contractors under a Status of Forces Agreement between the United States and Sri Lanka, those benefits or protections will be available to residents of the Contracting States regardless of any provisions to the contrary (or silence) in the Convention.

Paragraph 3

Paragraph 3 contains the traditional saving clause found in U.S. tax treaties. The Contracting States reserve their rights, except as provided in paragraph 4, to tax their residents and citizens as provided in their internal laws, notwithstanding any provisions of the Convention to the contrary. For example, if a resident of Sri Lanka performs independent personal services in the United States for less than 183 days within any 12-month period and the income from the services is not attributable to a fixed base in the United States, Article 15 (Independent Personal Services) would by its terms prevent the United States from taxing the income. If, however, the resident of Sri Lanka is also a citizen of the United States, the saving clause permits the United States to include the remuneration in the worldwide income of the citizen and subject it to tax under the normal Code rules (*i.e.*, without regard to Code section 894(a)).

For purposes of the saving clause, "residence" is determined under Article 4 (Resident). Thus, an individual who is a U.S. resident under the Internal Revenue Code but who is deemed to be a resident of Sri Lanka under the tie-breaker rules of Article 4 would be subject to U.S. tax only to the extent permitted by the Convention. For example, if an individual who is not a U.S. citizen is a resident of the United States under the Code, and is also a resident of Sri Lanka under its law, and the individual has a permanent home available to him in Sri Lanka and not in the United States, he would be treated as a resident of Sri Lanka under Article 4 and for purposes of the saving clause. The United States would not be permitted to apply its statutory rules to that person if they are inconsistent with the treaty.

However, the person would be treated as a U.S. resident for U.S. tax purposes other than determining the individual's U.S. tax liability. For example, in determining under Code section 957 whether a foreign corporation is a controlled foreign corporation, shares in that corporation held by the individual would be considered to be held by a U.S. resident. As a result, other U.S. citizens or residents might be deemed to be United States shareholders of a controlled foreign corporation subject to current inclusion of Subpart F income recognized by the corporation. *See* Treas. Reg. section 301.7701(b)-7(a)(3).

The application of the saving clause to former citizens and former long-term residents of a Contracting State. Each Contracting State reserves its right to tax former citizens and long-term residents whose loss of citizenship or long-term resident status had as one of its principal purposes the avoidance of tax. In the case of the United States, such a former citizen or long-term resident is taxable in accordance with the provisions of section 877 of the Code. Under section 877, the United States generally treats an individual as having a principal purpose to avoid tax if either of the following criteria exceed established thresholds: (a) the average annual net income tax of such individual for a period of 5 taxable years ending before the date of the loss of status, or (b) the net worth of such individual as of the date of the loss of status. These thresholds are adjusted annually for inflation. Section 877(c) provides certain exceptions to these presumptions of a tax avoidance purpose.

The United States defines "long-term resident" as an individual (other than a U.S. citizen) who is a lawful permanent resident of the United States in at least 8 of the 15 taxable years ending with the taxable year in which the individual ceased to be a long-term resident. An individual shall not be treated as a lawful permanent resident for any taxable year if such individual is treated as a resident of a foreign country under the provisions of a tax treaty between the United States and the foreign country and the individual does not waive the benefits of such treaty applicable to residents of the foreign country.

Paragraph 4

Some provisions of the Convention are intended to provide benefits to citizens and residents even if such benefits do not exist under internal law. Paragraph 4 sets forth certain exceptions to the saving clause that preserve these benefits for citizens and residents of the Contracting States.

Subparagraph (a) lists certain provisions of the Convention that are applicable to all citizens and residents of a Contracting State, despite the general saving clause rule of paragraph 3:

(1) Paragraph 2 of Article 9 (Associated Enterprises) grants the right to a correlative adjustment with respect to income tax due on profits reallocated under Article 9.

(2) Article 14 (Grants) covers grants provided by Sri Lanka in respect of an enterprise in Sri Lanka owned by a resident of the United States.

(3) Paragraphs 2 and 3 of Article 19 (Pensions, Social Security, and Child Support Payments) deal with social security benefits and child support payments, respectively. The inclusion of paragraph 2 in the exceptions to the saving clause means that the grant of exclusive taxing rights with respect to social security benefits to the paying country applies to deny, for example, to the United States the right to tax its citizens and residents on social security benefits paid by Sri Lanka. The inclusion of paragraph 3, which exempts child support payments from taxation by both States, means that if a resident of Sri Lanka pays child support to a citizen or resident of the United States, the United States may not tax the recipient on such payments.

(4) Article 24 (Relief from Double Taxation) confirms the benefit of a credit to citizens and residents of one Contracting State for income taxes paid to the other, even if such a credit may not be available under domestic law.

(5) Article 25 (Nondiscrimination) requires one Contracting State to grant national treatment to nationals of the other Contracting State in certain circumstances. The inclusion of this Article in the exceptions to the saving clause requires, for example, that the United States give such benefits to a national of Sri Lanka even if that person is a citizen of the United States.

(6) Article 26 (Mutual Agreement Procedure) may confer benefits on citizens and residents of the Contracting States. For example, the statute of limitations may be waived for refunds and the competent authorities are permitted to use a definition of a term that differs from the internal law definition. As with the foreign tax credit, these benefits are intended to be granted by a Contracting State to its citizens and residents.

Subparagraph (b) of paragraph 4 provides a different set of exceptions to the saving clause. The benefits referred to in subparagraph (b) are all intended to be granted to temporary residents of a Contracting State (for example, in the case of the United States, holders of non-immigrant visas), but not to citizens or to persons who have acquired permanent residence in that State. If beneficiaries of these provisions travel from one of the Contracting States to the other, and remain in the other long enough to become residents under its internal law, but do not acquire permanent residence status (*i.e.*, in the U.S. context, they do not become "green card" holders) and are not citizens of that State, the host State will continue to grant these benefits even if they conflict with internal law rules. The benefits preserved by this paragraph are the host country exemptions for the following items of income: government service salaries and pensions under Article 20 (Government Service); certain income of visiting students and trainees under Article 21 (Students and Trainees); and the income of diplomatic agents and consular officers under Article 28 (Diplomatic Agents and Consular Officers).

Paragraph 5

Paragraph 5 specifically relates to nondiscrimination obligations of the Contracting States under other agreements. The provisions of paragraph 5 are an exception to the rule provided in subparagraph (b) of paragraph 2 of this Article under which the Convention shall not restrict in any manner any exclusive exemption, deduction, credit or other allowance now or hereafter accorded by any other agreement between the Contracting States.

Subparagraph (a) of paragraph 5 provides that, notwithstanding any other agreement to which the Contracting States may be parties, a dispute concerning whether a measure is within the scope of this Convention shall be considered only by the competent authorities of the Contracting States, and the procedures under this Convention exclusively shall apply to the dispute. Thus, dispute-resolution procedures that may be incorporated into trade, investment, or other agreements between the Contracting States shall not apply for the purpose of determining the scope of the Convention.

Subparagraph (b) of paragraph 5 provides that, unless the competent authorities determine that a taxation measure is not within the scope of this Convention, the nondiscrimination obligations of this Convention exclusively shall apply with respect to that measure, except for such national treatment or most-favored-nation ("MFN") obligations as may apply to trade in goods under the General Agreement on Tariffs and Trade ("GATT"). No national treatment or MFN obligation under any other agreement shall apply with respect to that measure. Thus, unless the competent authorities agree otherwise, any national treatment and MFN obligations undertaken by the Contracting States under agreements other than the Convention shall not apply to a taxation measure, with the exception of GATT as applicable to trade in goods.

Subparagraph (c) of paragraph 3 defines a "measure" broadly. It includes, for example, a law, regulation, rule, procedure, decision, administrative action or any other form of governmental action or guidance.

Article 2 (Taxes Covered)

This Article identifies the U.S. and Sri Lankan taxes to which the Convention applies.

Paragraph 1

Paragraph 1 is based upon the OECD Model and defines the scope of application of the Convention. The Convention applies to taxes on income imposed on behalf of a Contracting State, irrespective of the manner in which they are levied. Except with respect to Article 25 (Nondiscrimination), state and local taxes are not covered by the Convention.

Paragraph 2

Paragraph 2 lists the taxes in force at the time of signature of the Convention to which the Convention applies.

Subparagraph 2(a) specifies the existing taxes of Sri Lanka that are covered by the Convention. In the case of Sri Lanka, the Convention applies to the income tax, including the income tax based on the turnover of enterprises licensed by the Greater Colombo Economic Commission.

Subparagraph 2(b) provides that the existing United States covered taxes are the Federal income taxes imposed by the Code. Subparagraph 2(b) excludes from coverage the accumulated earnings tax and the personal holding company tax. Under the Code, however, these taxes will not apply to most foreign corporations because of a statutory exclusion or the corporation's failure to meet a statutory requirement. In the few cases where the taxes may apply to a foreign corporation, the tax due is not likely to be significant.

Social security taxes (Code sections 1401, 3101, 3111 and 3301) also are specifically excluded from coverage even though they may be regarded as income taxes.

Paragraph 3

Paragraph 3 provides that the Convention will apply to any taxes that are substantially similar to those enumerated in paragraph 2, and which are imposed in addition to, or in place of, the existing taxes after the date of signature of the Convention. Paragraph 3 also provides that the U.S. and Sri Lankan competent authorities will notify each other of any significant changes in their taxation laws. The use of the term "significant" means that changes must be reported that are of significance to the operation of the Convention.

The competent authorities also are obligated to notify each other of official published materials concerning the application of the Convention. This requirement encompasses materials such as technical explanations, regulations, rulings and judicial decisions relating to the Convention.

Article 3 (General Definitions)

Paragraph 1

Paragraph 1 defines a number of basic terms used in the Convention. Certain others are defined in other articles of the Convention. For example, the term "resident of a Contracting State" is defined in Article 4 (Resident). The term "permanent establishment" is defined in Article 5 (Permanent Establishment). The terms "dividends," "interest" and "royalties" are defined in Articles 10, 11 and 12, respectively.

The introduction to paragraph 1 makes clear the definitions in Article 3 apply for all purposes of the Convention, unless the context requires otherwise. This latter condition allows the Convention to be interpreted in a manner that avoids unintended results. Terms that are not defined in the Convention are dealt with in paragraph 2.

Subparagraph (a) defines the term "Sri Lanka" to mean the Democratic Socialist Republic of Sri Lanka.

Subparagraph (b) defines the term "United States" to mean the United States of America, including the states, the District of Columbia and the territorial sea of the United States. The term does not include Puerto Rico, the Virgin Islands, Guam or any other U.S. possession or territory. Unlike the U.S. Model, the Convention does not explicitly include certain areas under the sea within the definition of the United States. However, the term "United States of America" is interpreted by reference to the U.S. internal law definition. Section 638 of the Code treats the continental shelf as part of the

United States. Therefore, the definition of "United States" is understood to extend to include the sea bed and subsoil of undersea areas adjacent to the territorial sea of the United States.

Subparagraph (c) states that the term "Contracting State" means the United States or Sri Lanka, as the context requires.

Subparagraph (d) defines the term "person" to include an individual, a partnership, a company, an estate, a trust, and any other body of persons. This definition is relevant for a variety of provisions. For example, under Article 4, only a "person" can be a "resident" and therefore eligible for most benefits under the treaty. Also, all "persons" are eligible to claim relief under Article 26 (Mutual Agreement Procedure).

The term "company" is defined in subparagraph (e) as any body corporate or any entity treated as a body corporate for tax purposes. Although the Convention does not add "in the state where it is organized," as does the U.S. Model, the result should be same as under the U.S. Model because the Commentary to Article 3 of the OECD Model interprets language identical to that of the Convention in a manner consistent with the U.S. Model.

The terms "enterprise of a Contracting State" and "enterprise of the other Contracting State" are defined in subparagraph (f) as an enterprise carried on by a resident of a Contracting State and an enterprise carried on by a resident of the other Contracting State. The term "enterprise" is not defined in the Convention, nor is it defined in the OECD Model or its Commentaries. The term is understood to refer to any activity or set of activities that constitute a trade or business.

Like the U.S. Model, subparagraph (f) provides that these terms also encompass an enterprise conducted through an entity (such as a partnership) that is treated as fiscally transparent in the Contracting State where the entity's owner is resident. This phrase has been included in order to address more explicitly some of the questions that can arise in the context of fiscally transparent entities. In accordance with Article 4 (Resident), entities that are fiscally transparent in the country in which their owners are resident are not considered to be residents of a Contracting State (although income derived by such entities may be taxed as the income of a resident, if taxed in the hands of resident partners or other owners). Given the approach taken in Article 4, an enterprise conducted by such an entity arguably might not qualify as an enterprise of a Contracting State under the OECD Model language which refers to an enterprise conducted by a resident, although most countries would attribute the enterprise to the owners of the entity in such circumstances. The definition in the Convention is intended to make clear that an enterprise conducted by such an entity will be treated as carried on by a resident of a Contracting State to the extent its partners or other owners are residents. This approach is consistent with the Code, which under section 875 attributes a trade or business conducted by a partnership to its partners and a trade or business conducted by an estate or trust to its beneficiaries.

An enterprise of a Contracting State need not be carried on in that State. It may be carried on in the other Contracting State or a third state (*e.g.*, a U.S. corporation doing all of its business in the other Contracting State would still be an enterprise of the United States).

Subparagraph (g) defines the term "international traffic." The term means any transport by a ship or aircraft except when the vessel is operated solely between places within the other Contracting State. This definition is applicable principally in the context of Article 8 (Shipping and Air Transport).

The exclusion from the definition of international traffic of transport by a ship or aircraft solely between places within a Contracting State means, for example, that carriage of goods or passengers solely between New York and Chicago would not be treated as international traffic, whether carried by a U.S. or a foreign carrier. The substantive taxing rules of the Convention relating to the taxation of income from transport, principally Article 8, therefore, would not apply to income from such carriage. Thus, if the carrier engaged in internal U.S. traffic were a resident of Sri Lanka (assuming that were possible under U.S. law), the United States would not be required to exempt the income from that transport under Article 8. The income would, however, be treated as business profits under Article 7 (Business Profits), and therefore would be taxable in the United States only if attributable to a U.S. permanent establishment of the foreign carrier, and then only on a net basis. The gross basis U.S. tax imposed by section 887 would never apply under the circumstances described.

If, however, goods or passengers are carried by a carrier resident in Sri Lanka from a non-U.S. port to, for example, New York, and some of the goods or passengers continue on to Chicago, the entire transport would be international traffic. This would be true even if the international carrier transferred the goods at the U.S. port of entry from a ship to a land vehicle, from a ship to a lighter, or even if the overland portion of the trip in the United States was handled by an independent carrier under contract with the original international carrier, so long as both parts of the trip were reflected in original bills of lading. For this reason, the Convention refers, in the definition of "international traffic," to "such transport" being solely between places in the other Contracting State, while the OECD Model refers to the ship or aircraft being operated solely between such places. The language of the Convention, based on U.S. Model language, is intended to make clear that, as in the above example, even if the goods are carried on a different aircraft for the internal portion of the international voyage than is used for the overseas portion of the trip, the definition applies to that internal portion as well as the external portion.

Finally, a "cruise to nowhere" (*i.e.*, a cruise beginning and ending in a port in the same Contracting State with no stops in a foreign port) would not constitute international traffic.

The term "national," as it relates to the United States and to Sri Lanka, is defined in subparagraph (h). This term is relevant for purposes of Articles 20 (Government

Service) and 25 (Nondiscrimination). In the case of the United States, a national is an individual who is a United States citizen, and, in the case of Sri Lanka, a national is an individual possessing the nationality of Sri Lanka. In the case of both Contracting States, a national is any legal person, partnership or association deriving its status, as such, from the law in force in the State where it is established.

Subparagraph (i) defines the term "competent authority" for Sri Lanka and the United States, respectively. The Sri Lankan competent authority is the Commissioner-General of Inland Revenue. The U.S. competent authority is the Secretary of the Treasury or his delegate. The Secretary of the Treasury has delegated the competent authority function to the Commissioner of Internal Revenue, who in turn has delegated the authority to the Director, International (LMSB). With respect to interpretative issues, the Director acts with the concurrence of the Associate Chief Counsel (International) of the Internal Revenue Service.

The definition of the term "qualified governmental entity" in subparagraph (j) is relevant for purposes of Articles 4 (Resident) and 23 (Limitation on Benefits). The term means:

(i)   The Government of a Contracting State or of a political subdivision or local authority of the Contracting State;

(ii)   A person that is wholly owned by a governmental entity described in subparagraph (i) and that satisfies certain organizational and funding standards; and

(iii)   A pension fund of a person that meets the standards of subparagraphs (i) and (ii) and that provides pension benefits described in Article 19 (Pensions, Social Security, And Child Support Payments).

A qualified governmental entity described in subparagraphs (ii) and (iii) may not engage in any commercial activity.

Paragraph 2

Paragraph 2 provides that in the application of the Convention, any term used but not defined in the Convention will have the meaning that it has under the law of the Contracting State whose tax is being applied, unless the context requires otherwise. The paragraph makes clear that if the term is defined under both the tax and non-tax laws of a Contracting State, the definition in the tax law will take precedence over the definition in the non-tax laws. Finally, there also may be cases where the tax laws of a State contain multiple definitions of the same term. In such a case, the definition used for purposes of the particular provision at issue, if any, should be used.

If the meaning of a term cannot be readily determined under the law of a Contracting State, or if there is a conflict in meaning under the laws of the two States that creates difficulties in the application of the Convention, the competent authorities, as indicated in paragraph 3(e) of Article 26 (Mutual Agreement Procedure), may establish a common meaning in order to prevent double taxation or to further any other purpose of the Convention. This common meaning need not conform to the meaning of the term under the laws of either Contracting State.

The reference in paragraph 2 to the internal law of a Contracting State means the law in effect at the time the treaty is being applied, not the law as in effect at the time the treaty was signed. The use of "ambulatory" definitions, however, may lead to results that are at variance with the intentions of the negotiators and of the Contracting States when the treaty was negotiated and ratified. The reference in both paragraphs 1 and 2 to the "context otherwise requir[ing]" a definition different from the treaty definition, in paragraph 1, or from the internal law definition of the Contracting State whose tax is being applied, under paragraph 2, refers to a circumstance where the result intended by the Contracting States is different from the result that would obtain under either the paragraph 1 definition or the statutory definition. This allows the Convention to be interpreted in a manner that avoids unintended results.

Article 4 (Resident)

This Article sets forth rules for determining whether a person is a resident of a Contracting State for purposes of the Convention. As a general matter only residents of the Contracting States may claim the benefits of the Convention. The treaty definition of residence is to be used only for purposes of the Convention. The fact that a person is determined to be a resident of a Contracting State under Article 4 does not necessarily entitle that person to the benefits of the Convention. In addition to being a resident, a person must also qualify for benefits under Article 23 (Limitation on Benefits) in order to receive benefits conferred on residents of a Contracting State.

The determination of residence for treaty purposes looks first to a person's liability to tax as a resident under the respective taxation laws of the Contracting States. A person who, under those laws, is a resident of one Contracting State and not of the other need look no further. That person is a resident for purposes of the Convention of the State in which he is resident under internal law. If, however, a person is a resident of both Contracting States under their respective taxation laws, the Article proceeds, where possible, to use tie-breaker rules to assign a single State of residence to such a person for purposes of the Convention.

Paragraph 1

The term "resident of a Contracting State" is defined in paragraph 1. In general, this definition incorporates the definitions of residence in U.S. and Sri Lankan law, by referring to a resident as a person who, under the laws of a Contracting State, is subject to tax there by reason of his domicile, residence, citizenship, place of management, place of incorporation or any other similar criterion. Thus, residents of the United States include aliens who are considered U.S. residents under Code section 7701(b). Subparagraphs (a) through (d) each address special cases that may arise in the context of Article 4.

Certain entities that are nominally subject to tax but that in practice are rarely required to pay tax also would generally be treated as residents and therefore accorded treaty benefits. For example, RICs, REITs and REMICs are all residents of the United States for purposes of the Convention. Although the income earned by these entities normally is not subject to U.S. tax in the hands of the entity, they are taxable to the extent that they do not currently distribute their profits, and therefore may be regarded as "liable to tax." They also must satisfy a number of requirements under the Code in order to be entitled to this special tax treatment.

Subparagraph (a) provides that a person who is liable to tax in a Contracting State only in respect of income from sources within that State will not be treated as a resident of that Contracting State for purposes of the Convention. Thus, a Sri Lankan consular official who is posted in the United States, who may be subject to U.S. tax on U.S. source investment income, but is not taxable in the United States on non-U.S. income, would not be considered a resident of the United States for purposes of the Convention (See Code section 7701(b)(5)(B)). Similarly, a Sri Lankan enterprise with a permanent establishment in the United States is not, by virtue of that permanent establishment, a resident of the United States. The enterprise generally is subject to U.S. tax only with respect to its income which is attributable to the U.S. permanent establishment, not with respect to its worldwide income as it would be if it were a U.S. resident.

Subparagraph (b) addresses the treatment of fiscally transparent entities such as partnerships and certain estates and trusts that are not subject to tax at the entity level. This subparagraph applies to any resident of a Contracting State who is entitled to income derived through an entity that is treated as fiscally transparent under the laws of either Contracting State. Entities falling under this description in the United States would include partnerships, common investment trusts under section 584, and grantor trusts. This paragraph also applies to U.S. limited liability companies ("LLC's") that are treated as partnerships for U.S. tax purposes.

Under subparagraph (b), an item of income, profit or gain derived through such fiscally transparent entities will be considered to be derived by a resident of a Contracting State if the resident is treated under the taxation laws of the State where he is resident as deriving the item of income. For example, if a Sri Lankan company pays interest to an entity that is treated as fiscally transparent for U.S. tax purposes, the interest will be considered to be derived by a resident of the United States only to the extent that the taxation laws of the United States treat one or more U.S. residents (whose status as U.S. residents is determined, for this purpose, under U.S. law) as deriving the interest for U.S. tax purposes. In the case of a partnership, the persons who are, under U.S. tax laws, treated as partners of the entity would normally be the persons whom the U.S. tax laws would treat as deriving the interest income through the partnership. Also, it follows that persons whom the United States treats as partners but who are not U.S. residents for U.S. tax purposes may not claim a benefit for the interest paid to the entity under the Convention, because they are not residents of the United States for purposes of claiming this treaty benefit. (If, however, the country in which they are treated as resident for tax purposes, as determined under the laws of that country, has an income tax convention with Sri Lanka, they may be entitled to claim a benefit under that convention.) In contrast, if, for example, an entity is organized under U.S. laws and is classified as a corporation for U.S. tax purposes, interest paid by a Sri Lankan company to such U.S. entity will be considered derived by a resident of the United States since the U.S. corporation is treated under U.S. taxation laws as a resident of the United States and as deriving the income.

The same result obtains even if the entity were viewed differently under the tax laws of Sri Lanka (*e.g.*, as not fiscally transparent in the first example above where the entity is treated as a partnership for U.S. tax purposes). Similarly, the characterization of the entity in a third country also is irrelevant, even if the entity is organized in that third country. These results follow regardless of whether the entity is disregarded as a separate entity under the laws of one jurisdiction but not the other, such as a single owner entity that is viewed as a branch for U.S. tax purposes and as a corporation for Sri Lankan tax purposes. These results also obtain regardless of where the entity is organized (*i.e.*, in the United States, in Sri Lanka, or, as noted above, in a third country).

For example, income from U.S. sources received by an entity organized under the laws of the United States, which is treated for Sri Lankan tax purposes as a corporation and is owned by a Sri Lankan shareholder who is a Sri Lankan resident for Sri Lankan tax purposes, is not considered derived by the shareholder of that corporation even if, under the tax laws of the United States, the entity is treated as fiscally transparent. Rather, for purposes of the Convention, the income is treated as derived by the U.S. entity.

These principles also apply to trusts to the extent that they are fiscally transparent in either Contracting State. For example, if X, a resident of Sri Lanka, creates a revocable trust in the United States and names persons resident in a third country as the beneficiaries of the trust, X would be treated under U.S. law as the beneficial owner of income derived from the United States. In that case, the trust's income would be regarded as being derived by a resident of Sri Lanka only to the extent that the laws of Sri Lanka treat X as deriving the income for Sri Lankan tax purposes.

Subparagraph 1(c) provides that certain tax-exempt entities such as pension funds and charitable organizations will be regarded as residents of the United States. An entity will be described in this subparagraph if it is generally exempt from tax by reason of the fact that it is organized and operated exclusively to perform a charitable or similar purpose or to provide pension or similar benefits to employees. The reference to "similar benefits" is intended to encompass employee benefits such as health and disability benefits.

The inclusion of this provision is intended to clarify the generally accepted practice of treating an entity that would be liable for tax as a resident under the internal law of a State but for a specific exemption from tax (either complete or partial) as a resident of that State for purposes of paragraph 1. The reference to a general exemption is intended to reflect the fact that, under U.S. law, certain organizations that generally are considered to be tax-exempt entities may be subject to certain excise taxes or to income

13

tax on their unrelated business income. Thus, a U.S. pension trust or a section 501(c) organization (such as a U.S. charity) that is generally exempt from tax under U.S. law is considered a resident of the United States for all purposes of the Convention.

Subparagraph 1(d) specifies that a qualified governmental entity (as defined in Article 3 (General Definitions)) is to be treated as a resident of the State where it is established.

Paragraph 2

If, under the laws of the two Contracting States, and, thus, under paragraph 1, an individual is deemed to be a resident of both Contracting States, a series of tie-breaker rules are provided in paragraph 2 to determine a single State of residence for that individual. These tests are to be applied in the order in which they are stated. The first test is based on where the individual has a permanent home. If that test is inconclusive because the individual has a permanent home available to him in both States, he will be considered to be a resident of the Contracting State where his personal and economic relations are closer (i.e., the location of his "center of vital interests"). If that test is also inconclusive, or if he does not have a permanent home available to him in either State, he will be treated as a resident of the Contracting State where he maintains an habitual abode. If he has an habitual abode in both States or in neither of them, he will be treated as a resident of the Contracting State of which he is a national. If he is a national of both States or of neither, the matter will be considered by the competent authorities, who will assign a single State of residence.

Paragraph 3

Dual resident companies are addressed in paragraph 3. If such a person is, under the rules of paragraph 1, a resident of both Contracting States, the residence of such company will be the Contracting State under the laws of which it is organized or created. For example, a company is treated as a resident of the United States if it is created or organized under the laws of the United States or a political subdivision. Under Sri Lankan law, a company is treated as a resident of Sri Lanka if it is either registered there, its principal office is there, or it is managed and controlled there. Dual residence, therefore, can arise in the case of a U.S. company is managed and controlled in Sri Lanka. Paragraph 3 provides that the residence of such a company will be the Contracting State under the laws of which it is created or organized (i.e., the United States in the example).

Paragraph 4

Dual residents other than individuals or companies (such as trusts or estates) are addressed in paragraph 4. If such a person is, under the rules of paragraph 1, a resident of both Contracting States, the competent authorities shall seek to determine a single State of residence for that person for purposes of the Convention.

Paragraph 5

Paragraph 5 provides that an individual who is a national of a Contracting State will be considered to be a resident of that State if certain requirements are met. First, the individual must be an employee of that State or an instrumentality thereof in the other Contracting State or a third state. Second, the individual must perform governmental functions for the first-mentioned State. Finally, the individual must be subject, in the first-mentioned State, to the same income tax obligations as are residents of that State. The spouse and minor children of an individual who meets the above requirements also will be considered to be residents of the first-mentioned State as long as they are, in their own right, subject to the same income tax obligations as are residents of the first-mentioned State.

Article 5 (Permanent Establishment)

This Article defines the term "permanent establishment," a term that is significant for several articles of the Convention. The existence of a permanent establishment in a Contracting State is necessary under Article 7 (Business Profits) for the taxation by that State of the business profits of a resident of the other Contracting State. Since the term "fixed base" in Article 15 (Independent Personal Services) is understood by reference to the definition of "permanent establishment," this Article is also relevant for purposes of Article 15. Articles 10, 11 and 12 (dealing with dividends, interest, and royalties, respectively) provide for reduced rates of tax at source on payments of these items of income to a resident of the other State only when the income is not attributable to a permanent establishment or fixed base that the recipient has in the source State. The permanent establishment concept is also relevant in determining which Contracting State may tax certain gains under Article 13 (Capital Gains) and certain "other income" under Article 22 (Other Income).

Paragraph 1

The basic definition of the term "permanent establishment" is contained in paragraph 1. As used in the Convention, the term means a fixed place of business through which the business of an enterprise is wholly or partly carried on. As indicated in the OECD Commentary to Article 4 (see paragraphs 4 through 8), a general principle to be observed in determining whether a permanent establishment exists is that the place of business must be fixed in the sense that a particular building or physical location is used by the enterprise for the conduct of its business and that it must be foreseeable that the enterprise's use of this building or other physical location will be more than temporary.

Paragraph 2

Paragraph 2 lists a number of types of fixed places of business that constitute a permanent establishment. This list is illustrative and non-exclusive. According to paragraph 2, the term permanent establishment includes a place of management, a branch, an office, a factory, a workshop, and a mine, oil or gas well, quarry or other place of extraction of natural resources. Each of these also is explicitly included in the U.S. Model.

Subparagraph (f) provides that a store or premises used as a sales outlet also constitutes a permanent establishment. While this type is not specifically provided for in the U.S. Model as a "fixed place of business through which the business of an enterprise is carried on," it is fully consistent with the principles of the Model and is, therefore, implicitly contained within the permanent establishment definition in the Model.

Paragraph 3

Subparagraph (a) provides rules to determine whether a building site or a construction or installation project or a drilling rig or ship used for the exploration of natural resources constitutes a permanent establishment for the contractor, installer, etc. Such an activity does not create a permanent establishment unless the site, project, etc. lasts for more than 183 days. It is only necessary to refer to "exploration" and not "exploitation" in this context because exploitation activities are defined to constitute a permanent establishment under subparagraph 2(g).

The 183-day test applies separately to each site or project. The 183-day period begins when work (including preparatory work carried on by the enterprise) physically begins in a Contracting State. A series of contracts or projects by a contractor that are interdependent both commercially and geographically are to be treated as a single project for purposes of applying the 183-day threshold test. For example, the construction of a housing development would be considered as a single project even if each house were constructed for a different purchaser.

In applying this paragraph, time spent by a sub-contractor on a building site is counted as time spent by the general contractor at the site for purposes of determining whether the general contractor has a permanent establishment. However, for the sub-contractor itself to be treated as having a permanent establishment, the sub-contractor's activities at the site must last for more then 183 days. If a sub-contractor is on a site intermittently, then, for purposes of applying the 183-day rule, time is measured from the first day the sub-contractor is on the site until the last day (*i.e.,* intervening days that the sub-contractor is not on the site are counted).

These interpretations of subparagraph (a) are based on the Commentary to paragraph 3 of Article 5 of the OECD Model, which contains language that is substantially the same as that in the Convention. These interpretations are consistent with the generally accepted international interpretation of the relevant language in subparagraph 3(a) of Article 5 of the Convention.

If the 183-day threshold is exceeded, the site or project constitutes a permanent establishment from the first day of activity.

Subparagraph 3(b) provides the rules for determining whether the furnishing of services by an enterprise through employees or other personnel constitutes a permanent establishment for the enterprise. Under the subparagraph, the furnishing of services gives rise to a permanent establishment if the activity continues for an aggregate of more than 183 days in a twelve month period. Under the U.S. Model, such activities would constitute a permanent establishment only if they are exercised through a fixed place of business or by a dependent agent.

Paragraph 4

This paragraph contains exceptions to the general rule of paragraph 1, listing a number of activities that may be carried on through a fixed place of business, but which nevertheless do not create a permanent establishment. The use of facilities solely to store, display or deliver merchandise belonging to an enterprise, other than goods or merchandise held for sale in a store or sales outlet, does not constitute a permanent establishment of that enterprise. The maintenance of a stock of goods belonging to an enterprise solely for the purpose of storage, display or delivery, or solely for the purpose of processing by another enterprise, other than goods or merchandise held for sale in a store or sales outlet, does not give rise to a permanent establishment of the first-mentioned enterprise. The maintenance of a fixed place of business solely for the purpose of purchasing goods or merchandise, or for collecting information, for the enterprise, or for other activities that have a preparatory or auxiliary character for the enterprise, such as advertising, or the supply of information, do not constitute a permanent establishment of the enterprise. Thus, as explained in paragraph 22 of the OECD Commentary to Article 5, a news bureau of a newspaper would not constitute a permanent establishment of the newspaper.

Subparagraph 4(f) provides that a combination of the activities described in the other subparagraphs of paragraph 4 will not give rise to a permanent establishment. This rule is different than the OECD Model, which requires that the overall combination of activities be of a preparatory or auxiliary character. The United States' position is that a combination of activities that are each preparatory or auxiliary always will result in an overall activity that is also preparatory or auxiliary.

Paragraph 5

Paragraph 5 specifies when activities carried on by agent on behalf of an enterprise create a permanent establishment of that enterprise. Under subparagraph 5(a), a dependent agent of an enterprise of a Contracting State is deemed to be a permanent establishment of the enterprise in the other Contracting State if the agent has and habitually exercises an authority to conclude contracts in the name of that enterprise. If, however, the agent's activities are limited to those activities specified in paragraph 4 that would not constitute a permanent establishment if carried on by the enterprise through a fixed place of business, the agent is not a permanent establishment of the enterprise.

The U.S. Model uses the phrase "binding on the enterprise" rather than "in the name of that enterprise" With reference to the conclusion of contracts. There is no substantive difference. As indicated in paragraph 32 to the OECD Commentary on Article 5, paragraph 5 is intended to encompass a person who has sufficient authority to bind the enterprise's participation in the business activity in the State concerned. It does not confine the application of the paragraph to an agent who enters contracts literally in the name of the enterprise.

The contracts referred to in subparagraph (a) are those relating to the essential business operations of the enterprise rather than ancillary activities. For example, if the agent has no authority to conclude contracts in the name of the enterprise with its customers for the sale of the goods produced by the enterprise, but it can enter into service contracts in the name of the enterprise for the enterprise's business equipment used in the agent's office, this contracting authority would not fall within the scope of the paragraph, even if exercised regularly.

Subparagraph 5(b) provides that an agent will be deemed to be a permanent establishment for an enterprise if the agent habitually maintains a stock of goods or merchandise in the other State on behalf of the enterprise and regularly makes deliveries from that stock, and there have been some additional activities carried on in that other State on behalf of the enterprise which have contributed to the sale. It is not necessary that the agent have authority to conclude contracts in the name of the enterprise. It is also not necessary that the sales activities be carried out by the agent. They may be carried out by the enterprise itself or by another agent.

Paragraph 6

Paragraph 6 provides that an insurance enterprise of one Contracting States will be deemed to have a permanent establishment in the other Contracting State if it collects premiums or insures risks in that other State through a person other than an independent agent as determined under paragraph 7.

Paragraph 7

Under paragraph 7, an enterprise is not deemed to have a permanent establishment in a Contracting State merely because it carries on business in that State through an independent agent, including a broker or general commission agent, if the agent is acting in the ordinary course of his business. Thus, there are two conditions that must be satisfied: the agent must be both legally and economically independent of the enterprise, and the agent must be acting in the ordinary course of its business in carrying out the activities on behalf of the enterprise

Whether the agent and the enterprise are independent is a factual determination. Among the questions to be considered is the extent to which the agent operates on the basis of instructions from the enterprise. An agent that is subject to detailed instructions regarding the conduct of its operations or comprehensive control by the enterprise is not legally independent. In determining whether the agent is economically independent, a relevant factor is the extent to which the agent bears business risk. Business risk refers primarily to risk of loss. An independent agent typically bears risk of loss from its own activities. In the absence of other factors that would establish dependence, an agent that shares business risk with the enterprise, or has its own business risk, is economically independent because its business activities are not integrated with those of the principal. Conversely, an agent that bears little or no risk from the activities it performs is not economically independent and therefore is not described in paragraph 6.

Another relevant factor in determining whether an agent is economically independent is whether the agent has an exclusive or nearly exclusive relationship with the principal. Such a relationship may indicate that the principal has economic control over the agent. A number of principals acting in concert also may have economic control over an agent. The limited scope of the agent's activities and the agent's dependence on a single source of income may indicate that the agent lacks economic independence. It should be borne in mind, however, that exclusivity is not in itself a conclusive test; an agent may be economically independent notwithstanding an exclusive relationship with the principal if it has the capacity to diversify and acquire other clients without substantial modifications to its current business and without substantial harm to its business profits. Thus, exclusivity should be viewed merely as a pointer to further investigation of the relationship between the principal and the agent. Each case must be addressed on the basis of its own facts and circumstances.

Notwithstanding the above, if the agent's activities are devoted wholly or almost wholly on behalf of the enterprise and transactions between the agent and the enterprise are on other than an arm's-length basis, the agent will not be considered an independent agent.

Paragraph 8

Paragraph 8 clarifies that a company that is a resident of a Contracting State is not deemed to have a permanent establishment in the other Contracting State merely because it controls, or is controlled by, a company that is a resident of that other Contracting State, or that carries on business in that other Contracting State. The determination of whether or not a permanent establishment exists will be made solely on the basis of the factors described in paragraphs 1 through 7 of the Article. Whether a company is a permanent establishment of a related company, therefore, is based solely on those factors and not on the ownership or control relationship between the companies.

Article 6 (Income From Immovable Property (Real Property))

Paragraph 1

The first paragraph of Article 6 states the general rule that income of a resident of a Contracting State derived from immovable (real) property situated in the other Contracting State may be taxed in the Contracting State in which the property is situated.

This Article does not grant an exclusive taxing right to the situs State; the situs State is merely given the primary right to tax. The Article does not include paragraph 5 of Article 6 of the U.S. Model, and therefore does not impose any limitation in terms of rate or form of tax on the situs State. However, both the United States and Sri Lanka allow non-residents to be taxed on income from real property on a net basis in the same manner as a resident.

Paragraph 2

The term "immovable property" is defined in paragraph 2 by reference to the internal law definition in the situs State. It is to be understood from the parenthetical use of the term "real property" in the title to the Article and in paragraph 1, that the term is synonymous with the term "immovable property" which is used in the OECD Model. In the case of the United States, the term has the meaning given to it by Reg. §1.897-1(b).

Paragraph 2 clarifies that real property includes, in any case, immovable property as described in the OECD Model, which includes references to accessory property, livestock and equipment used in agriculture and forestry, and rights to receive payments in exchange for the right to extract natural resources. Boats, ships and aircraft are not immovable property.

Paragraph 3

Paragraph 3 makes clear that all forms of income derived from the exploitation of real property are taxable in the Contracting State in which the property is situated. In the case of a net lease of real property, the gross rental payment (before deductible expenses incurred by the lessee) may be treated as income from the property. Income from the disposition of an interest in real property, however, is not considered "derived" from immovable property and is not dealt with in this Article. The taxation of that income is addressed in Article 13 (Capital Gains). Also, the interest paid on a mortgage on real property and distributions by a U.S. REIT are not dealt with in Article 6. Such payments would fall under Article 10 (Dividends), 11 (Interest) or 13 (Capital Gains). Finally, dividends paid by a United States Real Property Holding Corporation are not considered to be income from the exploitation of real property; such payments would fall under Article 10 (Dividends) or 13 (Capital Gains).

Paragraph 4

This paragraph specifies that the basic rule of paragraph 1 (as elaborated in paragraph 3) applies to income from real property of an enterprise and to income from real property used for the performance of independent personal services. This clarifies that the situs country may tax the real property income (including rental income) of a resident of the other Contracting State in the absence of attribution to a permanent establishment or fixed base in the situs State. This provision represents an exception to the general rule under Articles 7 (Business Profits) and 15 (Independent Personal

20

Services) that income must be attributable to a permanent establishment or fixed base, respectively, in order to be taxable in the host State.

Article 7 (Business Profits)

This Article provides rules for the taxation by a Contracting State of the business profits of an enterprise of the other Contracting State.

Paragraph 1

Paragraph 1 states the general rule that business profits of an enterprise of one Contracting State may not be taxed in the other Contracting State unless the enterprise carries on business in that other Contracting State through a permanent establishment (as defined in Article 5 (Permanent Establishment)) situated there. When this condition is met, the State in which the permanent establishment is situated may tax the enterprise on the income that is attributable to: (a) the permanent establishment; (b) sales in that State of goods or merchandise of the same or similar kind as those sold through the permanent establishment; or (c) other business activities carried on in that State of the same or similar kind as those effected through the permanent establishment. This limited force of attraction rule in paragraph 1 is similar to the rule in Article 7 of the U.N. Model. The rule in Article 7 of the U.S. Model is narrower, limiting the taxation of business profits to income attributable to a permanent establishment.

Although the Convention does not include a definition of the term "business profits," the term is intended to have the same meaning as under paragraph 7 of Article 7 of the U.S. Model. Thus, the term "business profits" generally means income from any trade or business. It would include income attributable to notional principal contracts and other financial instruments to the extent that the income is attributable to a trade or business of dealing in such instruments or is otherwise related to a trade or business (as in the case of a notional principal contract entered into for the purpose of hedging currency risk arising from an active trade or business). Any other income derived from such instruments is, unless specifically covered in another article, dealt with under Article 22 (Other Income).

Paragraph 2

Paragraph 2 provides rules for the attribution of business profits to a permanent establishment. The Contracting States will attribute to a permanent establishment the profits that it would have earned had it been an independent enterprise engaged in the same or similar activities under the same or similar circumstances. This language incorporates the arm's-length standard for purposes of determining the profits attributable to a permanent establishment. The computation of business profits attributable to a permanent establishment under this paragraph is subject to the rules of paragraph 3 for the allowance of expenses incurred for the purposes of earning the profits.

The "attributable to" concept of paragraph 2 is analogous but not entirely equivalent to the "effectively connected" concept in Code section 864(c). The profits attributable to a permanent establishment may be from sources within or without a Contracting State. Thus, certain items of foreign source income described in section 864(c)(4)(B) of the Code may be attributable to a U.S. permanent establishment of a Sri Lankan enterprise and subject to tax in the United States. However, the concept of "attributable to" in the Convention is narrower than the concept of "effectively connected" in section 864(c) of the Code. The limited "force of attraction" rule in Code section 864(c)(3), therefore, is not applicable under the Convention.

Paragraph 3

Paragraph 3 provides that in determining the business profits of a permanent establishment, deductions shall be allowed for the expenses incurred for the purposes of the permanent establishment, ensuring that business profits will be taxed on a net basis. This rule is not limited to expenses incurred exclusively for the purposes of the permanent establishment, but also includes a reasonable allocation of expenses incurred for the purposes of the enterprise as a whole, or that part of the enterprise that includes the permanent establishment. Deductions are to be allowed regardless of which accounting unit of the enterprise books the expenses, so long as they are incurred for the purposes of the permanent establishment. For example, a portion of the interest expense recorded on the books of the home office in one State may be deducted by a permanent establishment in the other State if properly allocable thereto.

The paragraph specifies that the expenses that may be considered to be incurred for the purposes of the permanent establishment are expenses for research and development, interest and other similar expenses, as well as a reasonable amount of executive and general administrative expenses. This rule permits (but does not require) each Contracting State to apply the type of expense allocation rules provided by U.S. law (such as Treas. Reg. §§1.861-8 and 1.882-5).

Paragraph 3 also states that a permanent establishment will not be permitted to deduct amounts it pays to the head office, or any other office, of the enterprise as royalties, fees or other similar payments in return for the use of patents, know-how or other rights, as commissions or other charges for specific services performed or for management, or as interest on moneys lent to the permanent establishment. Such payments made by the head office or any other office of the enterprise to a permanent establishment are similarly treated in determining the permanent establishment's profits. This provision is similar to the rule in Article 7(3) of the U.N. Model.

Paragraph 4

Paragraph 4 corresponds to paragraph 4 of Article 7 of the OECD Model and provides that a Contracting State in certain circumstances may determine the profits attributable to a permanent establishment on the basis of an apportionment of the total profits of the enterprise. A total profits method may be employed by a Contracting State if it has been customary in that State to use the method even though the figure may differ to some extent from a separate enterprise method so long as the result is in accordance with the principles of Article 7 (i.e., the application of the arm's length standard). Although this paragraph is not included in the U.S. Model, this is not a substantive difference because the result provided by paragraph 4 is consistent with the rest of Article 7.

The U.S. view is that paragraphs 2 and 3 of Article 7 authorize the use of total profits methods independently of paragraph 4 of Article 7 of the OECD Model because total profits methods are acceptable methods for determining the arm's length profits of affiliated enterprises under Article 9. Accordingly, it is understood that, under paragraph 2 of the Convention, it is permissible to use methods other than separate accounting to estimate the arm's length profits of a permanent establishment where it is necessary to do so for practical reasons, such as when the affairs of the permanent establishment are so closely bound up with those of the head office that it would be impossible to disentangle them on any strict basis of accounts. Any such approach, like any approach used under paragraph 4, is acceptable only if it approximates the result that would be achieved under an approach based on separate accounting. This view is confirmed by the OECD Commentary on paragraphs 2 and 3 of Article 7.

Paragraph 5

Paragraph 5 provides that no business profits can be attributed to a permanent establishment merely because it purchases goods or merchandise for the enterprise of which it is a part. This rule applies only to an office that performs functions for the enterprise in addition to purchasing. The income attribution issue does not arise if the sole activity of the permanent establishment is the purchase of goods or merchandise because such activity does not give rise to a permanent establishment under Article 5 (Permanent Establishment). A common situation in which paragraph 5 is relevant is one in which a permanent establishment purchases raw materials for the enterprise's manufacturing operation conducted outside the Contracting State in which the permanent establishment is located and then the permanent establishment sells the manufactured product. While business profits may be attributable to the permanent establishment with respect to its sales activities, no profits are attributable to it with respect to its purchasing activities.

Paragraph 6

Paragraph 6 provides that profits shall be determined by the same method each year, unless there is good reason to change the method used. This rule assures consistent tax treatment over time for permanent establishments. It limits the ability of both the Contracting State and the enterprise to change accounting methods to be applied to the permanent establishment. It does not, however, restrict a Contracting State from imposing additional requirements, such as the rules under Code section 481, to prevent amounts from being duplicated or omitted following a change in accounting method.

Paragraph 7

Paragraph 7 coordinates the provisions of Article 7 and other provisions of the Convention. Under this paragraph, when business profits include items of income that are dealt with separately under other articles of the Convention, the provisions of those articles will, except when they specifically provide to the contrary, take precedence over the provisions of Article 7. For example, the taxation of dividends will be determined by the rules of Article 10 (Dividends), and not by Article 7, except where, as provided in paragraph 6 of Article 10, the dividend is attributable to a permanent establishment. In the latter case the provisions of Article 7 apply. Thus, an enterprise of one State deriving dividends from the other State may not rely on Article 7 to exempt those dividends from tax at source if they are not attributable to a permanent establishment of the enterprise in the other State. By the same token, if the dividends are attributable to a permanent establishment in the other State, the dividends may be taxed on a net income basis at the source State full corporate tax rate, rather than on a gross basis under Article 10 (Dividends).

Paragraph 8

Paragraph 8 incorporates into the Convention the rule of Code section 864(c)(6). Like the Code section on which it is based, paragraph 8 provides that any income or gain attributable to a permanent establishment or a fixed base during its existence is taxable in the Contracting State where the permanent establishment or fixed base is situated, even if the payment of that income or gain is deferred until after the permanent establishment or fixed base ceases to exist. This rule applies with respect to paragraphs 1 and 2 of Article 7 (Business Profits), paragraph 4 of Article 10 (Dividends), paragraph 5 of Articles 11 (Interest) and 12 (Royalties), paragraph 3 of Article 13 (Capital Gains), and Article 15 (Independent Personal Services).

The effect of this rule can be illustrated by the following example. Assume a company that is a resident of Sri Lanka and that maintains a permanent establishment in the United States winds up the permanent establishment's business and sells the permanent establishment's inventory and assets to a U.S. buyer at the end of year 1 in exchange for an interest-bearing installment obligation payable in full at the end of year 3. Despite the fact that Article 13's threshold requirement for U.S. taxation is not met in year 3 because the company has no permanent establishment in the United States, the United States may tax the deferred income payment recognized by the company in year 3.

Relation to Other Articles

This Article is subject to the saving clause of paragraph 3 of Article 1 (Personal Scope). Thus, if a citizen of the United States who is a resident of Sri Lanka under the Convention derives business profits from the United States that are not attributable to a permanent establishment in the United States, the United States may tax those profits as part of the worldwide income of the citizen, notwithstanding the provision of paragraph 1 of this Article which would exempt the income from U.S. tax.

The benefits of this Article are also subject to Article 23 (Limitation on Benefits). Thus, an enterprise of Sri Lanka that derives income effectively connected with a U.S. trade or business may not claim the benefits of Article 7 unless the resident carrying on the enterprise qualifies for such benefits under Article 23.

Article 8 (Shipping and Air Transport)

This Article governs the taxation of profits from the operation of ships and aircraft in international traffic. The term "international traffic" is defined in subparagraph 1(g) of Article 3 (General Definitions). The taxation of gains from the alienation of ships, aircraft or containers is dealt with not in this Article, but in paragraph 4 of Article 13 (Gains).

Paragraph 1

Paragraph 1 provides that profits derived by an enterprise of a Contracting State from the operation of aircraft in international traffic are taxable only in that Contracting State. Because paragraph 7 of Article 7 (Business Profits) defers to Article 8 with respect to income from the operation of aircraft, such income derived by a resident of one of the Contracting States may not be taxed in the other State even if the enterprise has a permanent establishment in that other State. Thus, if a U.S. airline has a ticket office in Sri Lanka, Sri Lanka may not tax the airline's profits attributable to that office under Article 7.

Paragraph 2

Paragraph 2 provides for limited source-country taxation of income from the operation of ships in international traffic. Under this paragraph, the amount of tax that may be imposed by a Contracting State on profits derived by an enterprise of the other Contracting State from the operation of ships in international traffic shall be reduced to fifty percent of the amount which would have been imposed in the absence of the Convention. Thus, for example, under paragraph 2, the U.S. tax on the income of a Sri Lankan shipping company from the operation of ships in international traffic would be limited to a maximum of two percent of the company's U.S. source gross transportation income from such operation (under section 887 of the Code, the tax rate is four percent). In the case of Sri Lanka, paragraph 2 limits the Sri Lankan tax on shipping profits to the lesser of fifty percent of the amount otherwise due or six percent of the gross receipts from passengers or freight embarked in Sri Lanka.

Paragraph 2 is subject to paragraph 6 of Article 8, which further limits the amount of tax a Contracting State may impose under paragraph 2. The tax imposed by either Contracting State under paragraph 2 may not exceed the lowest rate that Sri Lanka imposes on profits of the same kind derived by a resident of a third state under any agreement with that third state. Sri Lanka has extended to other jurisdictions a full exemption for shipping income. Accordingly, the Notes clarify that the current effect of paragraph 6 is to grant a full exemption for income from the operation of ships in international traffic.

Paragraph 3

Paragraph 3 provides that income from the operation of aircraft in international traffic includes income from the rental of aircraft if the aircraft is operated in international traffic by the lessee or if such rental income is incidental to other profits described in paragraph 1. Thus, if a resident of the United States leases an aircraft to a resident of Sri Lanka, the lease payments will be exempt from tax in Sri Lanka either if the aircraft is used in international traffic by the resident of Sri Lanka, or if the U.S. lessor is engaged in the operation of aircraft in international traffic and the rental profits are incidental to such operation, regardless of whether the aircraft is used internationally or domestically by the lessee. Income from the rental of aircraft is incidental to income from the operation of aircraft in international traffic if the lessor is an airline and the aircraft is part of the body of equipment used by the lessor in its business as an international carrier. Such rental income is treated the same as income from the operation of aircraft under paragraph 1.

Paragraph 4

Paragraph 4 provides that incidental income of a resident of a Contracting State from the rental on a full (*i.e.*, with crew) or bareboat (*i.e.*, without crew) basis of ships operated by the lessee in international traffic may be taxable in both Contracting States, but the rate of tax imposed by the State of source may not exceed half of the rate of tax applied to royalties under paragraph 3 of Article 12 (Royalties) (*i.e.*, 2.5 percent).

Paragraph 4, like paragraph 2, is subject to paragraph 6 of this Article, which limits the amount of tax either Contracting State may impose under paragraph 4 to the lowest amount that Sri Lanka imposes under any agreement with a third state. Sri Lanka has extended to other jurisdictions a full exemption for shipping income, including the incidental income specified in paragraph 4. Accordingly, the Notes clarify that the current effect of paragraph 6 is to grant a full exemption for incidental income from the full or bareboat rental of ships operated by the lessee in international traffic. In addition, paragraph 5 of the Commentary to Article 8 of the OECD Model provides that "[p]rofits obtained by leasing a ship or aircraft on charter fully equipped, manned and supplied must be treated like the profits from the carriage or passengers or cargo." Accordingly, the combined effect of paragraph 6 and the exemption given by Sri Lanka to other countries is to exempt income from rentals on a full basis, whether or not the ship is used in international traffic by the lessee.

Paragraph 5

Under this paragraph, profits of an enterprise of a Contracting State from the use, maintenance or rental of containers (including equipment for their transport) that are used for the transport of goods or merchandise in international traffic are exempt from tax in the other Contracting State. This result obtains under paragraph 5 regardless of whether the recipient of the income is engaged in the operation of ships or aircraft in international traffic, and regardless of whether the enterprise has a permanent establishment in the other Contracting State.

Paragraph 6

Paragraph 6 states that Sri Lanka will provide to the United States most-favored-nation treatment with respect to shipping income. Sri Lanka has provided to third states a full exemption for such income in Sri Lanka's existing income tax conventions. Therefore, the Notes clarify that the same exemption extends to the United States on a most-favored-nation basis under paragraph 6.

Subparagraph 6(a) provides that tax imposed by either State under paragraph 2, regarding income from the operation of ships in international traffic, shall not exceed the amount of Sri Lankan tax that may be imposed on this type of income derived by a resident of a third State. Sri Lanka agreed to provide a full exemption for such income in Article 8(1) of the Convention between the Government of the Democratic Socialist Republic of Sri Lanka and the Government of the United Kingdom of Great Britain and Northern Ireland for the Avoidance of Double Taxation and the Prevention of Fiscal Evasion with Respect to Taxes on Income and Capital Gains, signed at London on June 21, 1979, and in Article 8(1) of the Convention Between the Government of the Polish People's Republic and the Government of the Democratic Socialist Republic of Sri Lanka for the Avoidance of Double Taxation and the Prevention of Fiscal Evasion with Respect to Taxes on Income and Capital, signed at Colombo on April 25, 1980. Accordingly, Sri Lanka acknowledged in the Notes that the same exemption for income from the operation of ships in international traffic extends to such income derived by an enterprise of the United States.

Subparagraph 6(b) states that the tax imposed by either Contracting State under paragraph 4, regarding rental income which is incidental to income described in paragraph 2, shall not exceed the amount of Sri Lankan tax that may be imposed on this type of income derived by a resident of a third State. The exemptions provided for shipping income in the Sri Lanka-United Kingdom and Sri Lanka-Poland conventions extend to this type of income. Accordingly, the Notes clarify that the current effect of paragraph 6 is to grant a full exemption for rental income which is incidental to income described in paragraph 2.

Paragraph 6 also states that the limitations imposed on Sri Lanka's ability to tax by subparagraphs 6(a) and 6(b) shall not apply on the basis of special domestic statutes applicable only to income derived by the government or governmental agency of a third

State. Because those limitations have been otherwise reduced to zero, as reflected in the Notes, this statement has no current effect.

Paragraph 7

Paragraph 7 clarifies that the provisions of paragraphs 1 through 6 also apply to profits derived by an enterprise of a Contracting State from participation in a pool, joint business or international operating agency of any kind by enterprises engaged in the operation of ships or aircraft in international traffic. This refers to various arrangements for international cooperation by carriers in shipping and air transport. For example, airlines from two countries may agree to share the transport of passengers between the two countries. They each will fly the same number of flights per week and share the revenues from that route equally, regardless of the number of passengers that each airline actually transports. Paragraph 7 makes clear that, with respect to each carrier, the Article applies to all income earned by the carrier with respect to the pool, and not just the income derived directly by that carrier. This paragraph corresponds to paragraph 4 of Article 8 of the U.S. Model.

Relation to Other Articles

This Article is subject to the saving clause of paragraph 3 of Article 1 (Personal Scope) of the Convention. Thus, if a citizen of the United States who is a resident of Sri Lanka derives profits from the operation of aircraft in international traffic, notwithstanding the exclusive residence country taxation in paragraph 1 of Article 8 (Shipping and Air Transport), the United States may tax those profits as part of the worldwide income of the citizen. (This is an unlikely situation, however, because non-tax considerations (*e.g.*, insurance) generally result in shipping activities being carried on in corporate form.)

As with other benefits of the Convention, the benefit of exclusive residence country taxation under Article 8 is available to an enterprise only if it is entitled to benefits under Article 23 (Limitation on Benefits).

Article 9 (Associated Enterprises)

This Article incorporates in the Convention the arms-length principle reflected in the U.S. domestic transfer pricing provisions, particularly Code section 482. It provides that when related enterprises engage in a transaction on terms that are not arm's-length, the Contracting States may make appropriate adjustments to the taxable income and tax liability of such related enterprises to reflect what the income and tax of these enterprises with respect to the transaction would have been had there been an arm's-length relationship between them.

Paragraph 1 addresses the situation where an enterprise of a Contracting State is related to an enterprise of the other Contracting State and there are arrangements or conditions imposed between the enterprises in their commercial or financial relations that are different from those that would have existed in the absence of the relationship. Under these circumstances, the Contracting States may adjust the income (or loss) of the enterprise to reflect what it would have been in the absence of such a relationship.

The paragraph identifies the relationships between enterprises that serve as a prerequisite to application of the Article. As the Commentary to Article 9 of the OECD Model makes clear, the necessary element in these relationships is effective control, which is also the standard for purposes of section 482. Thus, the Article applies if an enterprise of one State participates directly or indirectly in the management, control, or capital of the enterprise of the other State. Also, the Article applies if any third person or persons participate directly or indirectly in the management, control, or capital of enterprises of different States. For this purpose, all types of control are included (*i.e.,* whether or not legally enforceable and however exercised or exercisable.)

The fact that a transaction is entered into between such related enterprises does not, in and of itself, mean that a Contracting State may adjust the income (or loss) of one or both of the enterprises under the provisions of this Article. If the conditions of the transaction are consistent with those that would be made between independent persons, the income arising from that transaction should not be subject to adjustment under this Article.

Similarly, the fact that associated enterprises may have concluded arrangements, such as cost sharing arrangements or general services agreements, is not in itself an indication that the two enterprises have entered into a non-arm's-length transaction that should give rise to an adjustment under paragraph 1. Both related and unrelated parties enter into such arrangements (*e.g.,* joint venturers may share some development costs). As with any other kind of transaction, when related parties enter into an arrangement, the specific arrangement must be examined to see whether or not it meets the arm's-length standard. In the event that it does not, an appropriate adjustment may be made, which may include modifying the terms of the agreement or re-characterizing the transaction to reflect its substance.

It is understood that the "commensurate with income" standard for determining appropriate transfer prices for intangibles, added to Code section 482 by the Tax Reform Act of 1986, was designed to operate consistently with the arm's-length standard. The implementation of this standard in the section 482 regulations is in accordance with the general principles of paragraph 1 of Article 9 of the Convention, as interpreted by the OECD Transfer Pricing Guidelines.

This Article also permits tax authorities to deal with thin capitalization issues. They may, in the context of Article 9, scrutinize more than the rate of interest charged on a loan between related persons. They also may examine the capital structure of an enterprise, whether a payment in respect of that loan should be treated as interest, and, if it is treated as interest, under what circumstances interest deductions should be allowed to the payer. Paragraph 2 of the Commentary to Article 9 of the OECD Model, together with the U.S. observation set forth in paragraph 15 thereof, sets forth a similar understanding of the scope of Article 9 in the context of thin capitalization.

Paragraph 2

When a Contracting State has made an adjustment that is consistent with the provisions of paragraph 1, and the other Contracting State agrees that the adjustment was appropriate to reflect arm's-length conditions, that other Contracting State is obligated to make a correlative adjustment (sometimes referred to as a "corresponding adjustment") to the tax liability of the related person in that other Contracting State. Although the Convention, like the OECD Model, does not specify that the other Contracting State must agree with the initial adjustment before it is obligated to make the correlative adjustment, the Commentary to Article 9 of the OECD Model makes clear that the paragraph is to be read that way.

As explained in the OECD Commentary to Article 9, Article 9 leaves the treatment of "secondary adjustments" to the laws of the Contracting States. When an adjustment under Article 9 has been made, one of the parties will have in its possession funds that it would not have had at arm's length. The question arises as to how to treat these funds. In the United States the general practice is to treat such funds as a dividend or contribution to capital, depending on the relationship between the parties. Under certain circumstances, the parties may be permitted to restore the funds to the party that would have had the funds at arm's length, and to establish an account payable pending restoration of the funds. See Rev. Proc. 99-32, 1999-2 C.B. 296.

The Contracting State making a secondary adjustment will take the other provisions of the Convention, where relevant, into account. For example, if the effect of a secondary adjustment is to treat a U.S. corporation as having made a distribution of profits to its parent corporation in Sri Lanka, the provisions of Article 10 (Dividends) will apply, and the United States may impose a 15 percent withholding tax on the dividend. Also, if under Article 24 (Relief from Double Taxation) Sri Lanka generally gives a credit for taxes paid with respect to such dividends, it would also be required to do so in this case.

The competent authorities are authorized by paragraph 3 of Article 26 (Mutual Agreement Procedure) to consult, if necessary, to resolve any differences in the application of these provisions. For example, there may be a disagreement over whether an adjustment made by a Contracting State under paragraph 1 was appropriate.

If a correlative adjustment is made under paragraph 2, it is to be implemented, pursuant to paragraph 2 of Article 26 (Mutual Agreement Procedure), notwithstanding any time limits or other procedural limitations in the law of the Contracting State making the adjustment. If a taxpayer has entered a closing agreement (or other written settlement) with the United States prior to bringing a case to the competent authorities, the U.S. competent authority will endeavor only to obtain a correlative adjustment from the other Contracting State. See Rev. Proc. 2002-52, 2002-31 I.R.B. 242, Section 7.04.

Paragraph 3

Paragraph 3 provides that the Contracting States preserve their rights to apply internal law provisions relating to adjustments between related parties. They also reserve the right to make adjustments in cases involving tax evasion or fraud. Such adjustments -- the distribution, apportionment, or allocation of income, deductions, credits or allowances -- are permitted even if they are different from, or go beyond, those authorized by paragraph 1, as long as they accord with the general principles of paragraph 1 *(i.e.,* that the adjustment reflects what would have transpired had the related parties been acting at arm's length). For example, while paragraph 1 explicitly allows adjustments of deductions in computing taxable income, it does not deal with adjustments to tax credits. It does not, however, preclude such adjustments if they can be made under internal law. The OECD Model reaches the same result. See paragraph 4 of the Commentary to Article 9.

Relationship to Other Articles

The saving clause of paragraph 3 of Article 1 (Personal Scope) does not apply to paragraph 2 of Article 9 by virtue of the exceptions to the saving clause in paragraph 4(a) of Article 1. Thus, even if the statute of limitations has run, a refund of tax can be made in order to implement a correlative adjustment. Statutory or procedural limitations, however, cannot be overridden to impose additional tax, because paragraph 2 of Article 1 provides that the Convention cannot restrict any statutory benefit.

Article 10 (Dividends)

Article 10 provides rules for the taxation of dividends paid by a company that is a resident of one Contracting State to a beneficial owner that is a resident of the other Contracting State. The article provides for full residence-country taxation of such dividends and a limited source-State right to tax. Finally, the article prohibits a State from imposing taxes on dividends paid by companies resident in the other Contracting State and from imposing taxes, other than a branch profits tax, on undistributed earnings.

Article 12A provides rules for the imposition of a tax on branch profits by the State of source.

Paragraph 1

The right of a shareholder's country of residence to tax dividends arising in the other country is preserved by paragraph 1, which permits a Contracting State to tax its residents on dividends paid to them by a company that is a resident of the other

Contracting State. For dividends from any other source paid to a resident, Article 22 (Other Income) grants the residence country exclusive taxing jurisdiction (other than for dividends attributable to a permanent establishment or fixed base in the other State).

Paragraph 2

The State of source also may tax dividends beneficially owned by a resident of the other State, subject to the limitations in paragraph 2. Generally, the source State's tax is limited to 15 percent of the gross amount of the dividend paid.

Paragraph 2 also provides that this 15 percent maximum rate of withholding tax is applicable to dividends paid by a U.S. real estate investment trust only if one of three conditions is satisfied. First, the dividend may qualify for the 15 percent maximum rate of withholding tax if the beneficial owner of the dividend is an individual holding an interest in the REIT of not more than 10 percent. Second, the dividend may qualify for the 15 percent maximum rate of withholding tax if it is paid on a class of stock that is publicly traded and the beneficial owner of the dividends is a person holding an interest of not more than 5 percent of any class of the REIT's stock. Third, the dividend may qualify for the 15 percent maximum rate of withholding tax if the beneficial owner of the dividend is a person holding an interest in the REIT of not more than 10 percent and the value of no single interest in real property owned by the REIT exceeds 10 percent of the value of the REIT's total interest (*i.e.,* the REIT is diversified). If none of these conditions is met, dividends paid by the REIT will be subject to the U.S. domestic withholding rate of 30 percent.

The restrictions set forth above are intended to prevent the use of REITs to gain inappropriate source-country tax benefits for certain shareholder resident in the other Contracting State. For example, a resident of Sri Lanka directly holding U.S. real property would pay U.S. tax either at a 30-percent rate of withholding tax on the gross income or at graduated rates on the net income. By placing the real property in a REIT, the investor could transform real estate income into dividend income, taxable at the 15 percent withholding tax rate provided in Article 10, reducing the U.S. tax that otherwise would be imposed. Paragraph 2 prevents this result and thereby avoids disparity between the taxation of direct real estate investments and real estate investments made through REITs. In the cases covered by the exceptions, the holding in the REIT is not considered the equivalent of a direct holding in the underlying real property.

The benefits of paragraph 2 may be granted at the time of payment by means of reduced rate of withholding tax at source. It also is consistent with the paragraph for tax to be withheld at the time of payment at full statutory rates, and the treaty benefit to be granted by means of a subsequent refund so long as such procedures are applied in a reasonable manner.

Paragraph 2 does not affect the taxation of the profits out of which the dividends are paid. The taxation by a Contracting State of the income of its resident companies is governed by the internal law of the Contracting State, subject to the provisions of paragraph 4 of Article 25 (Nondiscrimination).

The term "beneficial owner" is not defined in the Convention, and is, therefore, defined as under the internal law of the country imposing the tax (*i.e.,* the source country). The beneficial owner of the dividend for purposes of Article 10 is the person to which the dividend income is attributable for tax purposes under the laws of the source State. Thus, if a dividend paid by a corporation that is a resident of one of the States (as determined under Article 4 (Resident)) is received by a nominee or agent that is a resident of the other State on behalf of the person that is not a resident of that other State, the dividend is not entitled to the benefits of this Article. However, a dividend received by a nominee on behalf of a resident of that other State would be entitled to benefits. These results are confirmed by paragraph 12 of the Commentary to Article 10 of the OECD Model. See also paragraph 24 of the Commentary to Article 1 of the OECD Model.

Companies holding shares through fiscally transparent entities such as partnerships are considered for purposes of this paragraph to hold their proportionate interest in the shares held by the intermediate entity.

Paragraph 3

Paragraph 3 defines the term "dividends" broadly. The definition is intended to cover all arrangements that yield a return on an equity investment in a corporation as determined under the tax law of the State of source, as well as arrangements that might be developed in the future.

The term "dividends" includes income from shares, mining shares, founders' shares or other corporate rights that are not treated as debt under the law of the source State, that participate in the profits of the company. The term also includes income that is subjected to the same tax treatment as income from shares by the law of the State of source. Thus, a constructive dividend that results from a non-arm's length transaction between a corporation and a related party is a dividend. Finally, a payment denominated as interest that is made by a thinly capitalized corporation may be treated as a dividend to the extent that the debt is recharacterized as equity under the laws of the source State.

In the case of the United States, the term dividend includes amounts treated as a dividend under U.S. law upon the sale or redemption of shares or upon a transfer of shares in a reorganization. See, *e.g.,* Rev. Rul. 92-85, 1992-2 C.B. 69 (sale of foreign subsidiary's stock to U.S. sister company is a deemed dividend to extent of subsidiary's and sister's earnings and profits). Further, a distribution from a U.S. publicly traded limited partnership, which is taxed as a corporation under U.S. law, is a dividend for purposes of Article 10. However, a distribution by a limited liability company is not characterized by the United States as a dividend and, therefore, is not a dividend for purposes of Article 10, provided the limited liability company is not characterized as an association taxable as a corporation under U.S. law.

Paragraph 4

Paragraph 4 excludes from the general limitations on source-country tax under paragraph 2 dividends paid with respect to holdings that form part of the business property of a permanent establishment or a fixed base situated in the source country. Such dividends will be taxed on a net basis using the rates and rules of taxation generally applicable to residents of the State in which the permanent establishment or fixed base is located, as modified by the Convention. An example of dividends paid with respect to the business property of a permanent establishment would be dividends derived by a dealer in stock or securities from stock or securities that the dealer held for sale to customers.

Relation to other Articles

The saving clause of paragraph 3 of Article 1 (Personal Scope) permits the United States to tax dividends received by its residents and citizens, notwithstanding the foregoing limitation on source country taxation of dividends.

The benefits of this Article are also subject to the provisions of Article 23 (Limitation on Benefits). Thus, if a resident of Sri Lanka is the beneficial owner of dividends paid by a U.S. company, the shareholder must qualify for treaty benefits under at least one of the tests of Article 23 in order to receive the benefits of this Article.

Article 11 (Interest)

Article 11 provides rules for the taxation of interest arising in one Contracting State and paid to a beneficial owner that is a resident of the other Contracting State.

Paragraph 1

Paragraph 1 generally grants to the State of residence the exclusive right to tax interest paid to its residents and arising in the other Contracting State.

Paragraph 2

The State of source also may tax interest beneficially owned by a resident of the other State, subject to the limitations in paragraph 2. Generally, the source State's tax is limited to 10 percent of the gross amount of the interest paid if the beneficial owner is a resident of the other Contracting State.

The term "beneficial owner" is not defined in the Convention, and is, therefore, defined under the internal law of the State of source. The beneficial owner of the interest for purposes of Article 11 is the person to which the interest income is attributable for tax purposes under the laws of the State of source. Thus, if interest arising in a Contracting State is received by a nominee or agent that is a resident of the other State on behalf of a person that is not a resident of that other State, the interest is not entitled to the benefits of Article 11. However, interest received by a nominee on behalf of a resident of that other

State would be entitled to benefits. These results are confirmed by paragraph 8 of the OECD Commentary to Article 11. See also paragraph 24 of the OECD Commentary to Article 1.

Paragraph 3

Paragraph 3 provides exceptions from the rule of paragraph 2 allowing source-country tax. The exceptions apply to interest that is included in any of three categories. The first category of interest that is exempt from tax in the source State is interest the payer of which is the Government of the source State, or a political subdivision or a local authority thereof. The second category of interest that is exempt from tax in the source State is interest that is derived and beneficially owned by the Government of the other Contracting State (including, in the case of the United States, the Export-Import Bank and the Overseas Private Investment Corporation). The third category of interest that is exempt from tax in the source State is interest paid to the Federal Reserve Banks of the United States or the Central Bank of Ceylon.

Paragraph 4

The term "interest" as used in Article 11 is defined in paragraph 4 to include, *inter alia*, income from debt claims of every kind, whether or not secured by a mortgage. Penalty charges for late payment are excluded from the definition of interest. Interest that is paid or accrued subject to a contingency is within the ambit of Article 11. This includes income from a debt obligation carrying the right to participate in profits. The term does not, however, include amounts that are treated as dividends under Article 10 (Dividends).

The term interest also includes amounts subject to the same tax treatment as income from money lent under the law of the State in which the income arises. Thus, for purposes of the Convention amounts that the United States will treat as interest include (i) the difference between the issue price and the stated redemption price at maturity of a debt instrument (*i.e.*, original issue discount (OID)), which may be wholly or partially realized on the disposition of a debt instrument (section 1273), (ii) amounts that are imputed interest on a deferred sales contract (section 483), (iii) amounts treated as interest or OID under the stripped bond rules (section 1286), (iv) amounts treated as original issue discount under the below-market interest rate rules (section 7872), (v) a partner's distributive share of a partnership's interest income (section 702), (vi) the interest portion of periodic payments made under a "finance lease" or similar contractual arrangement that in substance is a borrowing by the nominal lessee to finance the acquisition of property, (vii) amounts included in the income of a holder of a residual interest in a REMIC (section 860E), and (viii) interest with respect to notional principal contracts that are recharacterized as loans because of a "substantial non-periodic payment."

Paragraph 5

Paragraph 5 provides exceptions to the limitations on source-country tax in paragraphs 2 and 3 for three classes of interest payments.

Subparagraph (a) of paragraph 5 allows source-country taxation of interest in cases where the beneficial owner of the interest carries on business through a permanent establishment in the State of source or performs independent personal services from a fixed base situated in that State and the interest is attributable to that permanent establishment or fixed base. In such cases the provisions of Article 7 (Business Profits) or Article 14 (Independent Personal Services) will apply and the State of source will retain the right to impose tax on such interest income.

In the case of a permanent establishment or fixed base that once existed in the State but that no longer exists, the provisions of subparagraph (a) also apply, by virtue of paragraph 8 of Article 7 (Business Profits), to interest that would be attributable to such a permanent establishment or fixed base if it did exist in the year of payment or accrual. See the Technical Explanation of paragraph 8 of Article 7.

The second exception, in subparagraph (b) of paragraph 5, is consistent with the policy of Code sections 860E(e) and 860G(b) that excess inclusions with respect to a real estate mortgage investment conduit (REMIC) should bear full U.S. tax in all cases. Without a full tax at source foreign purchasers of residual interests would have a competitive advantage over U.S. purchasers at the time these interests are initially offered. Also, absent this rule the U.S. fisc would suffer a revenue loss with respect to mortgages held in a REMIC because of opportunities for tax avoidance created by differences in the timing of taxable and economic income produced by these interests.

Subparagraph (c) deals with contingent interest of a type that does not qualify as portfolio interest under United States law, whether arising in the United States or Sri Lanka. Under this provision, contingent interest arising in one of the Contracting States that is determined by reference to the receipts, sales, income, profits or other cash flow of the debtor or a related person, to any change in the value of any property of the debtor or a related person or to any dividend, partnership distribution or similar payment made by the debtor or a related person, and that is paid to a resident of the other State, also may be taxed in the Contracting State in which it arises, and according to the laws of that State. If the beneficial owner of such interest is a resident of the other Contracting State, the gross amount of the interest may be taxed at a rate not exceeding 15 percent.

Paragraph 6

Paragraph 6 provides a source rule for interest. It provides that interest shall be deemed to arise in a Contracting State when the payer is that State itself or a political subdivision, local authority, or resident of that State. The exception to the general rule that interest is sourced in the State of the payer's residence is the case in which the payer of the interest, whether a resident of a Contracting State or not, is subject to tax on a net basis in the other State (either because it carries on business through a permanent establishment in the other State, performs independent personal services from a fixed base situated in the other State, or is subject to tax under Article 6 (Income from Immovable Property (Real Property)) or Article 13 (Capital Gains)) and the interest is borne by the activity subject to net basis taxation. In such cases, the interest will be deemed to arise in that other State.

Paragraph 7

Paragraph 7 provides that, in cases involving special relationships between persons, Article 11 applies only to that portion of the total interest payments between those persons that would have been made absent such special relationships (*i.e.,* an arm's-length interest payment). Any excess amount of interest paid remains taxable according to the laws of the United States and Sri Lanka, respectively, with due regard to the other provisions of the Convention. Thus, if the excess amount would be treated under the source country's law as a distribution of profits by a corporation, such amount would be taxed as a dividend rather than as interest, but the tax would be subject, if appropriate, to the rate limitations of Article 10 (Dividends).

The term "special relationship" is not defined in the Convention. In applying this paragraph the United States considers the term to include the relationships described in Article 9 (Associated Enterprises), which in turn correspond to the definition of "control" for purposes of section 482 of the Code.

This paragraph does not address cases where, owing to a special relationship between the payer and the beneficial owner or between both of them and some other person, the amount of the interest is less than an arm's-length amount. In those cases a transaction may be characterized to reflect its substance and interest may be imputed consistent with the definition of interest in paragraph 2. Consistent with Article 9 (Associated Enterprises), the United States would apply section 482 or 7872 of the Code to determine the amount of imputed interest in those cases.

Relation to Other Articles

The saving clause of paragraph 3 of Article 1 (Personal Scope) permits the United States to tax its residents and citizens, notwithstanding the foregoing limitations on source country taxation of interest.

The benefits of this Article are also subject to the provisions of Article 23 (Limitation on Benefits). Thus, if a resident of Sri Lanka is the beneficial owner of interest paid by a U.S. corporation, the shareholder must qualify for treaty benefits under at least one of the tests of Article 23 in order to receive the benefits of this Article.

Article 12 (Royalties)

Article 12 provides rules for the taxation of royalties arising in one Contracting State and paid to a beneficial owner that is a resident of the other Contracting State.

Paragraph 1

Paragraph 1 generally grants to the State of residence the exclusive right to tax royalties paid to its residents and arising in the other Contracting State.

Paragraph 2

Paragraph 2 provides an exception to exclusive residence-State taxation in the case of certain royalties. However, if the beneficial owner of such royalties is a resident of the other Contracting State, the source State shall not impose a tax that exceeds 10 percent of the gross amount of the royalties.

The term "beneficial owner" is not defined in the Convention, and is, therefore, defined under the internal law of the State of source. The beneficial owner of the royalty for purposes of Article 12 is the person to which the royalty income is attributable for tax purposes under the laws of the State of source. Thus, if a royalty arising in a Contracting State is received by a nominee or agent that is a resident of the other State on behalf of a person that is not a resident of that other State, the royalty is not entitled to the benefits of Article 12. However, a royalty received by a nominee on behalf of a resident of that other State would be entitled to benefits. These results are confirmed by paragraph 4 of the OECD Commentary to Article 12. See also paragraph 24 of the OECD Commentary to Article 1.

Paragraph 3

Paragraph 3 provides an exception to exclusive residence-State taxation in the case of rentals for the use of tangible personal property. However, if the beneficial owner of such rentals is a resident of the other Contracting State, the source State may not impose a tax that exceeds 5 percent of the gross amount of the rentals.

Paragraph 4

Paragraph 4 defines the term "royalties" as used in Article 12.

Subparagraph (a) provides that the term includes payments of any kind received as a consideration for the use of, or the right to use, any copyright of a literary, artistic, scientific or other work; for the use of, or the right to use, any patent, trademark, design or model, plan, secret formula or process, or other like right or property; or for information concerning industrial, commercial, or scientific experience.

Subparagraph (b) provides that the term "royalties" includes rentals for the use of tangible personal property.

The term royalties is defined in the Convention and therefore is generally independent of domestic law. Certain terms used in the definition are not defined in the Convention, but these may be defined under domestic tax law. For example, the term "secret process or formulas" is found in the Code, and its meaning has been elaborated in the context of sections 351 and 367. See Rev. Rul. 55-17, 1955-1 C.B. 388; Rev. Rul. 64-56, 1964-1 C.B. 133; Rev. Proc. 69-19, 1969-2 C.B. 301.

Consideration for the use of or right to use cinematographic films, or works on film, tape, or other means of reproduction in radio or television broadcasting is specifically included in the definition of royalties. It is intended that, with respect to any subsequent technological advances in the field of radio or television broadcasting, consideration received for the use of such technology will also be included in the definition of royalties.

If an artist who is resident in one Contracting State records a performance in the other Contracting State, retains a copyrighted interest in a recording, and receives payments for the right to use the recording based on the sale or public playing of the recording, then the right of such other Contracting State to tax those payments is governed by Article 12. See Boulez v. Commissioner, 83 T.C. 584 (1984), aff'd, 810 F.2d 209 (D.C. Cir. 1986). By contrast, if the artist earns in the other Contracting State income covered by Article 18 (Entertainers and Athletes), such as, for example, endorsement income from the artist's attendance at a film screening, and if such income also is attributable to one of the rights described in Article 12 (*e.g.*, the use of the artist's photograph in promoting the screening), Article 16 and not Article 12 is applicable to such income.

Computer software generally is protected by copyright laws around the world. Under the Convention, consideration received for the use of, or the right to use, computer software is treated either as royalties or as business profits, depending on the facts and circumstances of the transaction giving rise to the payment.

The primary factor in determining whether consideration received for the use of, or the right to use, computer software is treated as royalties or as business profits is the nature of the rights transferred. See Treas. Reg. section 1.861-18. The fact that the transaction is characterized as a license for copyright law purposes is not dispositive. For example, a typical retail sale of "shrink wrap" software generally will not be considered to give rise to royalty income, even though for copyright law purposes it may be characterized as a license.

The means by which the computer software is transferred are not relevant for purposes of the analysis. Consequently, if software is electronically transferred but the rights obtained by the transferee are substantially equivalent to rights in a program copy, the payment will be considered business profits.

The term "industrial, commercial, or scientific experience" (sometimes referred to as "know-how") has the meaning ascribed to it in paragraph 11 of the Commentary to Article 12 of the OECD Model. Consistent with that meaning, the term may include information that is ancillary to a right otherwise giving rise to royalties, such as a patent or secret process.

Know-how also may include, in limited cases, technical information that is conveyed through technical or consultancy services. It does not include general educational training of the user's employees, nor does it include information developed especially for the user, such as a technical plan or design developed according to the user's specifications. Thus, as provided in paragraph 11 of the Commentary to Article 12 of the OECD Model, the term "royalties" does not include payments received as consideration for after-sales service, for services rendered by a seller to a purchaser under a guarantee, or for pure technical assistance.

The term "royalties" also does not include payments for professional services (such as architectural, engineering, legal, managerial, medical, or software development services). For example, income from the design of a refinery by an engineer (even if the engineer employed know-how in the process of rendering the design) or the production of a legal brief by a lawyer is not income from the transfer of know-how taxable under Article 12, but is income from services taxable under either Article 7 (Business Profits) or Article 14 (Income from Employment). Professional services may be embodied in property that gives rise to royalties, however. Thus, if a professional contracts to develop patentable property and retains rights in the resulting property under the development contract, subsequent license payments made for those rights would be royalties.

Paragraph 5

Paragraph 5 provides an exception to rules of paragraphs 2 and 3 that limit the rate of source country taxation of royalties. This paragraph applies in cases where the beneficial owner of the royalties carries on business through a permanent establishment in the State of source or performs independent personal services from a fixed base situated in that State and the royalties are attributable to that permanent establishment or fixed base. In such cases the provisions of Article 7 (Business Profits) or Article 15 (Independent Personal Services) will apply.

The provisions of paragraph 8 of Article 7 (Business Profits) apply for purposes of this paragraph. For example, royalty income that is attributable to a permanent establishment or a fixed base and that accrues during the existence of the permanent establishment or fixed base, but is received after the permanent establishment or fixed base no longer exists, remains taxable under the provisions of Articles 7 (Business Profits) or 15 (Independent Personal Services), respectively, and not under this Article.

Paragraph 6

Paragraph 6 provides a source rule for royalties.

With respect to royalties defined in subparagraph 4(a), subparagraph (a) of paragraph 6 provides generally that such royalties are deemed to arise in a Contracting State if paid by a resident of that State, including the State itself or a political subdivision or local authority thereof. However, where the right or property for which the royalties are paid is used within the United States, the royalties are deemed to arise in the United States to the extent of such use.

Subparagraph (b) of paragraph 6 provides that royalties defined in subparagraph 4(b) are deemed to arise in a Contracting State to the extent the property for which the royalties are paid is used within the Contracting State.

Paragraph 7

Paragraph 4 provides that in cases involving special relationships between the payer and beneficial owner of royalties, Article 12 applies only to the extent the royalties would have been paid absent such special relationships (i.e., an arm's-length royalty). Any excess amount of royalties paid remains taxable according to the laws of the two Contracting States with due regard to the other provisions of the Convention. If, for example, the excess amount is treated as a distribution of corporate profits under domestic law, such excess amount will be taxed as a dividend rather than as royalties, but the tax imposed on the dividend payment will be subject to the rate limitations of paragraph 2 of Article 10 (Dividends).

Relation to Other Articles

The saving clause of paragraph 3 of Article 1 (Personal Scope) permits the United States to tax its residents and citizens, notwithstanding the foregoing limitations on source country taxation of royalties.

The benefits of this Article are also subject to the provisions of Article 23 (Limitation on Benefits). Thus, if a resident of Sri Lanka is the beneficial owner of royalties paid by a U.S. corporation, the shareholder must qualify for treaty benefits under at least one of the tests of Article 23 in order to receive the benefits of this Article.

Article 12A (Branch Tax)

Paragraph 1

Paragraph 1 permits a State to impose a branch profits tax on a company resident in the other State. The tax is in addition to other taxes permitted by the Convention. Since the term "company" is not defined in the Convention, it will be defined for this purpose under the law of the host State.

Paragraph 2

Clause (i) of subparagraphs (a) and (b) permits the United States and Sri Lanka, respectively, to impose a branch profits tax on a company resident in the other State if the company has income attributable to a permanent establishment in the first-mentioned State, derives income from real property in the first-mentioned State that is taxed on a net basis under Article 6, or realizes gains taxable in the first-mentioned State under paragraph 1 of Article 13. The tax is limited, however, to the aforementioned items of income that are included in the "dividend equivalent amount."

Clause (ii) of subparagraphs (a) and (b) permits the United States and Sri Lanka, respectively, to impose branch taxes on the excess interest of a company resident in the other State which derives business profits attributable to a permanent establishment in the first-mentioned State or which derives income subject to tax on a net basis in the first-mentioned State under Articles 6 or 13.

The term "dividend equivalent amount" used in paragraph 2 has the same meaning that it has under section 884 of the Code, as amended from time to time, provided the amendments are consistent with the purpose of the branch profits tax. Generally, the dividend equivalent amount for a particular year is the income described above that is included in the corporation's effectively connected earnings and profits for that year, after payment of the corporate tax under Articles 6, 7 or 13, reduced for any increase in the branch's U.S. net equity during the year and increased for any reduction in its U.S. net equity during the year. U.S. net equity is U.S. assets less U.S. liabilities. See Treas. Reg. section 1.884-1. The dividend equivalent amount for any year approximates the dividend that a U.S. branch office would have paid during the year if the branch had been operated as a separate U.S. subsidiary company. In the case that the other Contracting State also imposes a branch profits tax, the base of its tax must be limited to an amount that is analogous to the dividend equivalent amount.

Excess interest is generally the portion of the entire enterprise's interest expense that is allocated to the branch over the amount of interest paid by the branch to third parties. The excess amount is deemed paid to the head office, and a tax is applied to the amount of that deemed payment. Such excess interest is treated under Article 11 as arising from the Contracting State in which the branch is located because it is borne by the permanent establishment.

Neither Contracting State may impose a branch profits tax on the business profits of a company resident in the other State that are effectively connected with a trade or business in that Contracting State but that are not attributable to a permanent establishment and are not otherwise subject to in that State under Article 6 or paragraph 1 of Article 13.

Paragraph 3

Subparagraph (a) provides that the branch profits tax imposed by the United States or Sri Lanka under subparagraphs (a)(i) and (b)(i) of paragraph 2 on the dividend equivalent amount shall be imposed at a rate not to exceed 15 percent.

Subparagraph (b) provides that the branch tax imposed by the United States or Sri Lanka under subparagraphs (a)(ii) and (b)(ii) of paragraph 2 on excess interest shall be imposed at a rate not to exceed 10 percent.

Article 13 (Capital Gains)

Article 13 assigns either primary or exclusive taxing jurisdiction over gains from the alienation of property to the State of residence or the State of source and defines the terms necessary to apply the Article.

Paragraph 1

Paragraph 1 of Article 13 preserves the non-exclusive right of the State of source to tax gains attributable to the alienation of real property situated in that State. The paragraph therefore permits the United States to apply section 897 of the Code to tax gains derived by a resident of Sri Lanka that are attributable to the alienation of real property situated in the United States (as defined in paragraph 2). Gains attributable to the alienation of real property include gain from any other property that is treated as a real property interest within the meaning of paragraph 2.

Paragraph 2

This paragraph defines the term "real property situated in the other Contracting State."

Under subparagraph (a), the term "real property situated in the other Contracting State" includes both real property referred to in Article 6 (i.e., an interest in the real property itself) and a "United States real property interest," when the United States is the other Contracting State under paragraph 1. The "United States real property interest" includes shares in a U.S. company that owns sufficient U.S. real property interests to satisfy an asset-ratio test on certain testing dates. See I.R.C. §897(c). The term "United States real property interest" also encompasses an interest in a foreign company that has elected to be treated as a U.S. company for this purpose. See I.R.C. §897(i). The term also includes an interest in a partnership, trust or estate to the extent the assets of the partnership, trust or estate consist of property situated in the United States or of an interest referred to in the preceding sentence. In applying paragraph 1 the United States will look through capital gain distributions made by a REIT. Accordingly, distributions made by a REIT are taxable under paragraph 1 of Article 13 (not under Article 10 (Dividends)) when they are attributable to gains derived from the alienation of real property.

Under subparagraph (b), the term "real property situated in the other Contracting State" includes, when Sri Lanka is the other Contracting State, real property referred to in Article 6 (*i.e.,* an interest in the real property itself) and an interest in a company the assets of which consist, directly or indirectly, principally of real property referred to in Article 6. The term also includes an interest in a partnership, trust or estate to the extent the assets of the partnership, trust or estate consist of property situated in Sri Lanka, or of an interest referred to in the preceding sentence.

Paragraph 3

Paragraph 3 of Article 13 deals with the taxation of certain gains from the alienation of property, other than real property, forming part of the business property of a permanent establishment that an enterprise of a Contracting State has in the other Contracting State or of property, other than real property, pertaining to a fixed base available to a resident of a Contracting State in the other Contracting State for the purpose of performing independent personal services. This also includes gains from the alienation of such a permanent establishment (alone or with the whole enterprise) or of such fixed base. Such gains may be taxed in the State in which the permanent establishment or fixed base is located.

A resident of Sri Lanka that is a partner in a partnership doing business in the United States generally will have a permanent establishment in the United States as a result of the activities of the partnership, assuming that the activities of the partnership rise to the level of a permanent establishment. Rev. Rul. 91-32, 1991-1 C.B. 107. Further, under paragraph 3, the United States generally may tax a partner's distributive share of income realized by a partnership on the disposition of personal (movable) property forming part of the business property of the partnership in the United States.

Paragraph 4

This paragraph limits the taxing jurisdiction of the State of source with respect to gains from the alienation of ships or aircraft operated in international traffic by the enterprise alienating the ship or aircraft, from containers used in international traffic, and from property (other than real property) pertaining to the operation or use of such ships, aircraft, or containers.

Under paragraph 4, such income is taxable only in the Contracting State in which the alienator is resident. Notwithstanding paragraph 3, the rules of this paragraph apply even if the income is attributable to a permanent establishment maintained by the enterprise in the other Contracting State. This result is consistent with the allocation of taxing rights under Article 8 (Shipping and Air Transport).

Paragraph 5

Under paragraph 5, gains derived by a resident of a Contracting State from the sale of shares of a company, which is a resident of the other Contracting State, representing a participation of 50 percent or more may be taxed in the State in which the company is a resident.

Paragraph 6

This paragraph provides that gains described in Article 12 (Royalties) are taxable only under Article 12. Accordingly, gains derived from the alienation of any property, such as a patent or copyright, that produces income taxable under Article 12 is taxable under Article 12 and not under this Article, provided that such gain is of the type described in paragraph 4(a) of Article 12 (i.e., it is contingent on the productivity, use, or disposition of the property).

Paragraph 7

Paragraph 7 grants to the State of residence of the alienator the exclusive right to tax gains from the alienation of property other than property referred to in paragraphs 1 through 6. For example, gain derived from shares (other than shares described in paragraph 2 or 5, debt instruments, and various financial instruments may be taxed only in the State of residence, to the extent such income is not otherwise characterized as income taxable under another article (e.g., Article 10 (Dividends) or Article 11 (Interest)). Similarly, gain derived from the alienation of tangible personal property, other than tangible personal property described in paragraph 3, may be taxed only in the State of residence of the alienator. Sales by a resident of a Contracting State of real property located in a third state are not taxable in the other Contracting State, even if the sale is attributable to a permanent establishment located in the other Contracting State.

Relation to other Articles

The saving clause of paragraph 3 of Article 1 (Personal Scope) permits the United States to tax its citizens and residents, notwithstanding the foregoing limitations on taxation of certain gains by the State of source. Thus, any limitation in this Article on the right of the United States to tax gains does not apply to gains of a U.S. citizens or resident.

The benefits of this Article are also subject to the provisions of Article 23 (Limitation on Benefits). Thus, only a resident of a Contracting State that satisfies one of the conditions in Article 23 is entitled to the benefits of this Article.

Article 14 (Grants)

This Article details the manner in which Sri Lankan governmental grants to U.S. residents will be treated for U.S. tax purposes. This Article confirms, with some clarifying detail, the result which would obtain under U.S. law in the absence of the Convention. This provision is not found in the U.S. Model or the OECD Model, but a similar provision is contained in Article 10 (Grants) of the U.S.-Israel Income Tax Convention.

Paragraph 1

Paragraph 1 provides that for the purpose of computing United States tax, if Sri Lanka or any agency thereof makes a cash grant or any similar payment to a United States resident in respect of a wholly owned enterprise or company in Sri Lanka, then the amount of such grant will be excluded from the gross income of such resident or company and will not increase the earnings and profits of such resident or company. *Paragraph 2*

Paragraph 2 specifies additional U.S. income tax consequences to certain recipients of a grant or payment described in paragraph 1. If the recipient is a U.S. resident that is a company, then the amount of the grant will be treated as a contribution to its capital. The U.S. resident will be considered to have contributed the amount of such grant to the Sri Lankan corporation designated by the terms of the grant, and the resident's basis for the stock of the Sri Lankan corporation will not be increased by the amount of the contributed grant. The basis of the assets of the Sri Lankan corporation will be reduced by the amount of the deemed contribution, in accordance with rules prescribed by the Secretary of the Treasury.

The Convention has no special provision with respect to a U.S. resident who acquires assets directly from the proceeds of a grant. Thus, for example, if the U.S. resident is a corporation, the rules of section 362(c) of the Code will apply and the U.S. resident will be required to reduce its basis in certain assets acquired after the contribution.

Paragraph 3

Paragraph 3 specifies additional U.S. income tax consequences to certain grant recipients not described in paragraph 2. If Sri Lanka or its agency makes the grant or payment directly to a Sri Lankan company wholly owned by a U.S. resident, as described in paragraph 1, then the amount of the grant or payment will be treated as a contribution to the capital of the Sri Lankan company, and the basis of the assets of the Sri Lankan corporation will be reduced by the amount of the deemed contribution. [New]

Paragraph 4

Paragraph 4 limits the types of grants or payments that may qualify for treatment under paragraph 1. A qualifying grant will not include any amount which in whole or part, directly or indirectly, is in consideration for services rendered or to be rendered or for the sale of goods; is measured in any manner by the amount of profits or tax liability of the investor or the Sri Lankan corporation in which the investment is made; or which is taxed by Sri Lanka. These requirements generally are consistent with section 118 of the Code, regarding non-shareholder contributions to capital, and the regulations thereunder.

Paragraph 5 provides for an election by a U.S. resident who receives a grant or payment described in paragraph 1 to include such grant or payment in income. If he so elects, and the grant is included in income, Article 14 (Grants) would not apply, and the U.S. resident would increase his basis in the stock of the Sri Lankan corporation by the amount of the grant. [Israel/New]

Article 15 (Independent Personal Services)

The Convention deals in separate articles with different classes of income from personal services. Article 15 deals with the general class of income from independent personal services and Article 16 deals with the general class of income from dependent personal services. Articles 17 through 21 provide exceptions and additions to these general rules for directors' fees (Article 17); performance income of artistes and athletes (Article 18); pensions in respect of personal service income, social security benefits, and child support payments (Article 19); government service income (Article 20); and certain income of students and trainees (Article 21).

Paragraph 1

Paragraph 1 of Article 15 provides the general rule that an individual who is a resident of a Contracting State and who derives income from performing personal services in an independent capacity will be exempt from tax in respect of that income by the other Contracting State. The income may be taxed in the other Contracting State only if the services are performed there and (a) the individual is present in that other State for a period of more than 183 days in any 12-month period; or (b) the income is attributable to a fixed base that is regularly available to the individual in that other State for the purpose of performing his services.

Income derived by persons other than individuals or groups of individuals from the performance of independent personal services is not covered by Article 15. Such income generally would be business profits taxable in accordance with Article 7 (Business Profits). Income derived by employees of such persons generally would be taxable in accordance with Article 16 (Dependent Personal Services).

The term "fixed base" is not defined in the Convention, but its meaning is understood to be similar, but not identical, to that of the term "permanent establishment," as defined in Article 5 (Permanent Establishment). The term "regularly available" also is not defined in the Convention. Whether a fixed base is regularly available to a person will be determined based on all the facts and circumstances. In general, the term encompasses situations where a fixed base is at the disposal of the individual whenever he performs services in that State. It is not necessary that the individual regularly use the fixed base, only that the fixed base be regularly available to him. For example, a U.S. resident partner in a law firm that has offices Sri Lanka would be considered to have a fixed base regularly available to him in Sri Lanka if the law firm had an office in Sri Lanka that was available to him whenever he wished to conduct business in the other State, regardless of how frequently he conducted business in the other State. On the other hand, an individual who had no office in the other State and occasionally rented a hotel room to serve as a temporary office would not be considered to have a fixed base regularly available to him.

It is not necessary that the individual actually use the fixed base. It is only necessary that the fixed base be regularly available to him. For example, if an individual has an office in the other State that he can use if he chooses when he is present in the other State, that fixed base will be considered to be regularly available to him regardless of whether he conducts his activities there.

The taxing right conferred by this Article with respect to income from independent personal services can be more limited than that provided in Article 7 for the taxation of business profits. In both articles the income of a resident of one Contracting State must be attributable to a permanent establishment or fixed base in the other State in order for that other State to have a taxing right. In Article 15 the income also must be attributable to services performed in that other State, while Article 7 does not require that all of the income generating activities be performed in the State where the permanent establishment is located.

The term "personal services of an independent character" is not defined. It clearly includes those activities listed in paragraph 2 of Article 14 of the OECD Model, such as independent scientific, literary, artistic, educational or teaching activities, as well as the independent activities of physicians, lawyers, engineers, architects, dentists, and accountants. That list, however, is not exhaustive. The term includes all personal services performed by an individual for his own account, whether as a sole proprietor or a partner, where he receives the income and bears the risk of loss arising from the services. The taxation of income of an individual from those types of independent services which are covered by Articles 16 through 20 is governed by the provisions of those articles. For example, taxation of the income of a professional musician would be governed by Article 18 (Artistes and Athletes) rather than Article 15.

This Article applies to income derived by a partner resident in a Contracting State that is attributable to personal services performed in the other Contracting State through a partnership with a fixed base in that other State.

The application of Article 15 to a service partnership may be illustrated by the following example: a partnership formed in Sri Lanka has five partners (who agree to split profits equally), four of whom are resident and perform services only in Sri Lanka at Office A, and one of whom performs personal services at Office B, a fixed base in the United States. In this case, the four partners of the partnership resident in Sri Lanka may be taxed in the United States in respect of their share of income attributable to the fixed base in the United State, Office B. The services giving rise to income which may be attributable to the fixed base would include not only the services performed by the one resident partner, but also, for example, if one of the four other partners came to the United States and worked on an Office B matter there, the income in respect of those services. Income from the services performed by the visiting partner would be subject to tax in the United States regardless of whether the visiting partner actually visited or used Office B while performing services in the United States.

Paragraph 8 of Article 7 (Business Profits) refers to Article 15. That rule clarifies that income that is attributable to a permanent establishment or a fixed base, but that is deferred and received after the permanent establishment or fixed base no longer exists, may nevertheless be taxed by the State in which the permanent establishment or fixed base was located. Thus, under Article 15, income derived by an individual resident of a Contracting State from services performed in the other Contracting State and attributable to a fixed base there may be taxed by that other State even if the income is deferred and received after there is no longer a fixed base available to the resident in that other State.

If an individual resident of the other Contracting State who is also a U.S. citizen performs independent personal services in the United States, the United States may, by virtue of the saving clause of paragraph 3 of Article 1 (Personal Scope), tax his income without regard to the restrictions of this Article, subject to the special foreign tax credit rules of Article 23 (Relief from Double Taxation).

Article 16 (Dependent Personal Services)

Article 16 apportions taxing jurisdiction over remuneration derived by a resident of a Contracting State as an employee between the States of source and residence.

Paragraph 1

The general rule of Article 16 is contained in paragraph 1. Remuneration derived by a resident of a Contracting State as an employee may be taxed by the State of residence, and the remuneration also may be taxed by the other Contracting State to the extent derived from employment exercised (*i.e.*, services performed) in that other Contracting State. Paragraph 1 also provides that the more specific rules of Articles 18 (Artistes and Athletes), 19 (Pensions, Social Security, and Child Support Payments), and 20 (Government Service) apply in the case of employment income described in one of those articles. Thus, even though the State of source has a right to tax employment income under Article 16, it may not have the right to tax that income under the Convention if the income is described, for example, in Article 19 (Pensions, Social Security, and Child Support Payments) and is not taxable in the State of source under the provisions of that article.

The Convention refers to "other remuneration." This language was intended to make clear that Article 16 applies to any form of compensation for employment, including payments in kind, regardless of whether the remuneration is "similar" to salaries and wages. The interpretation of Article 16 to include in kind payments is reflected in the addition of paragraph 2.1 to the Commentaries to Article 15 of the OECD Model.

Consistent with section 864(c)(6), Article 16 also applies regardless of the timing of actual payment for services. Thus, a bonus paid to a resident of a Contracting State with respect to services performed in the other Contracting State with respect to a particular taxable year would be subject to Article 16 for that year even if it was paid after the close of the year. Similarly, an annuity received for services performed in a taxable year would be subject to Article 16 despite the fact that it was paid in subsequent years. In either case, whether such payments were taxable in the State where the employment was exercised would depend on whether the tests of paragraph 2 were satisfied. Consequently, a person who receives the right to a future payment in consideration for services rendered in a Contracting State would be taxable in that State even if the payment is received at a time when the recipient is a resident of the other Contracting State.

Paragraph 2

Paragraph 2 sets forth an exception to the general rule that employment income may be taxed in the State where it is exercised. Under paragraph 2, the State where the employment is exercised may not tax the income from the employment if three conditions are satisfied: (1) the individual is present in the other Contracting State for a period or periods not exceeding 183 days in any 12-month period; (2) the remuneration is paid by, or on behalf of, an employer who is not a resident of that other Contracting State; and (3) the remuneration is not borne as a deductible expense by a permanent establishment or fixed base that the employer has in that other State. In order for the remuneration to be exempt from tax in the source State, all three conditions must be satisfied. This exception is similar to that set forth in the U.S. and OECD Models.

The 183-day period in condition (a) is to be measured using the "days of physical presence" method. Under this method, the days that are counted include any day in which a part of the day is spent in the host country. See Rev. Rul. 56-24, 1956-1 C.B. 851. Thus, days that are counted include the days of arrival and departure; weekends and holidays on which the employee does not work but is present within the country; vacation days spent in the country before, during or after the employment period, unless the individual's presence before or after the employment can be shown to be independent of his presence there for employment purposes; and time during periods of sickness, training periods, strikes, etc., when the individual is present but not working. If illness prevented the individual from leaving the country in sufficient time to qualify for the benefit, those days will not count. Also, any part of a day spent in the host country while in transit between two points outside the host country is not counted. These rules are consistent with the description of the 183-day period in paragraph 5 of the Commentary to Article 15 in the OECD Model.

Conditions (b) and (c) are intended to ensure that a Contracting State will not be required to allow a deduction to the payer for compensation paid and at the same time to exempt the employee on the amount received. Accordingly, if a foreign person pays the salary of an employee who is employed in the host State, but a host State corporation or permanent establishment reimburses the payer with a payment that can be identified as a reimbursement, neither condition (b) nor (c), as the case may be, will be considered to have been fulfilled.

The reference to remuneration "borne by" a permanent establishment or fixed base is understood to encompass all expenses that economically are incurred and not merely expenses that are currently deductible for tax purposes. Accordingly, the expenses referred to include expenses that are capitalizable as well as those that are currently deductible. Further, salaries paid by residents that are exempt from income taxation may be considered to be borne by a permanent establishment or fixed base notwithstanding the fact that the expenses will be neither deductible nor capitalizable since the payer is exempt from tax.

Article 16 contains a special rule applicable to remuneration for services performed as an employee aboard a ship or aircraft operated in international traffic by an enterprise of a Contracting State. Under this paragraph, the employment income of a member of the regular complement of a ship or aircraft may be taxed only in the State of residence of the enterprise operating the ship or aircraft. The "regular complement" includes the crew. In the case of a cruise ship, for example, it may also include others, such as entertainers, lecturers, etc., employed by the shipping company to serve on the ship throughout its voyage. The use of the term "regular complement" is intended to clarify that a person who exercises his employment as, for example, an insurance salesman while aboard a ship or aircraft is not covered by this paragraph. This paragraph does not apply to persons dealt with in Article 15 (Independent Personal Services).

U.S. internal law does not impose tax on non-U.S. source income of a person who is neither a U.S. citizen nor a U.S. resident, even if that person is an employee of a U.S. resident enterprise. Thus, under U.S. internal law, the United States will not tax the salary of a resident of Sri Lanka who is employed by a U.S. carrier and who is not a U.S. citizen or resident, except as provided in paragraph 2.

Relation with other Articles

Notwithstanding the foregoing limitations on taxation of certain income by the State of source the saving clause of paragraph 3 of Article 1 (Personal Scope) permits the Untied States to tax its citizens and residents as if the Convention had not come into effect. Thus, any limitation in this Article on the right of the United States to tax income from employment does not apply to income of a U.S. citizen or resident.

Article 17 (Directors' Fees)

This Article provides that a Contracting State may tax the fees and other compensation paid by a company that is a resident of that State for services performed in that State by a resident of the other Contracting State as a director of the company. This rule is an exception to the more general rules of Article 15 (Independent Personal Services) and Article 16 (Dependent Personal Services). Thus, for example, in determining whether a director's fee paid to a non-employee director is subject to tax in the country of residence of the company, it is not relevant to establish whether the fee is attributable to a fixed base in that State.

The analogous OECD provision reaches a different result in certain cases. Under the OECD Model provision, a resident of one Contracting State who is a director of a company that is resident in the other Contracting State is subject to tax in that other State in respect of his directors' fees regardless of where the services are performed. The United States has entered a reservation with respect to the OECD Model provision. Under this Convention, the State of residence of the company may tax nonresident directors with no time or dollar threshold, but only with respect to remuneration for services performed in that State.

The Convention refers to "other compensation." This language was intended to make clear that Article 17 applies to any form of compensation, including payments in kind, regardless of whether the remuneration is "similar" to director's fees. This language was used even though it is no longer necessary because of a recent addition to the Commentary to Article 16 of the OECD Model; paragraph 1.1 now confirms that payments in kind are covered by the Article.

Relation to other Articles

Article 17 is subject to the saving clause of paragraph 3 of Article 1 (Personal Scope). Thus, if a U.S. citizen who is a resident of Sri Lanka is a director of a U.S. corporation, the United States may tax his full remuneration regardless of where he performs his services.

Article 18 (Artistes and Athletes)

This Article deals with the taxation in a Contracting State of entertainers (i.e., performing artists) and athletes resident in the other Contracting State from the performance of their services as such. The Article applies both to the income of an entertainer or athlete who performs services on his own behalf and one who performs services on behalf of another person, either as an employee of that person, or pursuant to any other arrangement. The rules of this Article take precedence, in some circumstances, over those of Articles 15 (Independent Personal Services) and 16 (Dependent Personal Services)

This Article applies only with respect to the income of entertainers and athletes. Others involved in a performance or athletic event, such as producers, directors, technicians, managers, coaches, etc., remain subject to the provisions of Articles 15 and 16. In addition, except as provided in paragraph 2, income earned by juridical persons is not covered by Article 18.

Paragraph 1

Paragraph 1 describes the circumstances in which a Contracting State may tax the performance income of an entertainer or athlete who is a resident of the other Contracting State. Under the paragraph, income derived by an individual resident of a Contracting State from activities as an entertainer or athlete exercised in the other Contracting State may be taxed in that other State if the amount of the gross receipts derived by the performer exceeds $6,000 (or its equivalent in Sri Lanka rupees) for the taxable year. The $6,000 includes expenses reimbursed to the individual or borne on his behalf. If the gross receipts exceed $6,000, the full amount, not just the excess, may be taxed in the State of performance.

The OECD Model provides for taxation by the country of performance of the remuneration of entertainers or athletes with no dollar or time threshold. The United States includes the dollar threshold test in its treaties to distinguish between two groups of entertainers and athletes -- those who are paid very large sums of money for very short periods of service and who would, therefore, normally be exempt from host country tax under the standard personal services income rules, and those who earn relatively modest amounts and are, therefore, not easily distinguishable from those who earn other types of personal service income. The United States has entered a reservation to the OECD Model on this point.

Tax may be imposed under paragraph 1 even if the performer would have been exempt from tax under Articles 15 (Independent Personal Services) or 16 (Dependent Personal Services). On the other hand, if the performer would be exempt from host-country tax under Article 18, but would be taxable under either Article 15 or 16, tax may be imposed under either of those Articles. Thus, for example, if a performer derives remuneration from his activities in an independent capacity, and the remuneration is not attributable to a fixed base in the host State, he may be taxed by the host State in accordance with Article 18 if his remuneration exceeds $6,000 annually, despite the fact that he generally would be exempt from host State taxation under Article 15. Moreover, a performer who receives less than the $6,000 threshold amount and therefore is not taxable under Article 18, nevertheless may be subject to tax in the host country under Articles 15 or 16 if the tests for host-country taxability under the relevant Article are met. For example, if an entertainer who is an independent contractor earns $5,000 of income in a State for the calendar year, but the income is attributable to a fixed base regularly available to him in the State of performance, that State may tax his income under Article 15.

Since it frequently is not possible to know until year-end whether the income an entertainer or athlete derived from a performance in a Contracting State will exceed $6,000, nothing in the Convention precludes that Contracting State from withholding tax during the year and refunding it after the close of the year if the taxability threshold has not been met.

As explained in paragraph 9 of the Commentary to Article 17 of the OECD Model, Article 18 of the Convention applies to all income connected with a performance by the entertainer, such as appearance fees, award or prize money, and a share of the gate receipts. Income derived from a Contracting State by a performer who is a resident of the other Contracting State from other than actual performance, such as royalties from record sales and payments for product endorsements, is not covered by this Article, but by other articles of the Convention, such as Article 12 (Royalties) or Article 15 (Independent Personal Services). For example, if an entertainer receives royalty income from the sale of live recordings, the royalty income could be taxed by the source country under Article 12 and he could also be taxed in the source country with respect to income from the performance itself under Article 18 if the dollar threshold is exceeded.

In determining whether income falls under Article 18 or another article, the controlling factor will be whether the income in question is predominantly attributable to the performance itself or other activities or property rights. For instance, a fee paid to a performer for endorsement of a performance in which the performer will participate would be considered to be so closely associated with the performance itself that it normally would fall within Article 18. Similarly, a sponsorship fee paid by a business in return for the right to attach its name to the performance would be so closely associated with the performance that it would fall under Article 18 as well. As indicated in paragraph 9 of the Commentary to Article 17 of the OECD Model, a cancellation fee would not be considered to fall within Article 18 but would be dealt with under Article 7 (Business Profits), 15 (Independent Personal Services) or 16 (Dependent Personal Services).

As indicated in paragraph 4 of the Commentary to Article 17 of the OECD Model, where an individual fulfills a dual role as performer and non-performer (such as a player-coach or an actor-director), but his role in one of the two capacities is negligible, the predominant character of the individual's activities should control the characterization of those activities. In other cases there should be an apportionment between the performance-related compensation and other compensation.

Consistent with Article 16 (Dependent Personal Services), Article 18 also applies regardless of the timing of actual payment for services. Thus, a bonus paid to a resident of a Contracting State with respect to a performance in the other Contracting State with respect to a particular taxable year would be subject to Article 18 for that year even if it was paid after the close of the year.

Paragraph 2

Paragraph 2 of the Article provides an exception to the rules in paragraph 1 in the case of a visit to a Contracting State by an entertainer or athlete who is a resident of the other Contracting State, if the visit is wholly or mainly supported by the public funds of his State of residence or of a political subdivision or local authority of that State. In that case, only the Contracting State of which the entertainer or athlete is a resident may tax his income from those services.

Paragraph 3

Paragraph 3 is intended to deal with the potential for abuse when a performer's income does not accrue directly to the performer himself, but to another person. Foreign performers frequently perform in the United States as employees of, or under contract with, a company or other person.

The relationship may truly be one of employee and employer, with no abuse of the tax system either intended or realized. On the other hand, the "employer" may, for example, be a company established and owned by the performer, which is merely acting as the nominal income recipient in respect of the remuneration for the performance (a "star company"). The performer may act as an "employee," receive a modest salary, and arrange to receive the remainder of the income from his performance in another form or at a later time. In such case, absent the provisions of paragraph 3, the income arguably could escape host-country tax because the company earns business profits but has no permanent establishment in that country. The performer may largely or entirely escape host-country tax by receiving only a small salary in the year the services are performed, perhaps small enough to place him below the dollar threshold in paragraph 1. The performer might arrange to receive further payments in a later year, when he is not subject to host-country tax, perhaps as deferred salary payments, dividends or liquidating distributions.

Paragraph 3 seeks to prevent this type of abuse while at the same time protecting the taxpayers' rights to the benefits of the Convention when there is a legitimate employee-employer relationship between the performer and the person providing his services. Under paragraph 3, when the income accrues to a person other than the performer, and the performer or related persons participate, directly or indirectly, in the receipts or profits of that other person, the income may be taxed in the Contracting State where the performer's services are exercised, without regard to the provisions of the Convention concerning business profits (Article 7) or independent personal services (Article 15). Thus, even if the "employer" has no permanent establishment or fixed base in the host country, its income may be subject to tax there under the provisions of paragraph 3. Taxation under paragraph 3 is on the person providing the services of the performer. This paragraph does not affect the rules of paragraph 1, which apply to the performer himself. The income taxable by virtue of paragraph 3 is reduced to the extent of salary payments to the performer, which fall under paragraph 1.

For purposes of paragraph 3, income is deemed to accrue to another person (i.e., the person providing the services of the performer) if that other person has control over, or the right to receive, gross income in respect of the services of the performer. Direct or indirect participation in the profits of a person may include, but is not limited to, the accrual or receipt of deferred remuneration, bonuses, fees, dividends, partnership income or other income or distributions.

Paragraph 3 does not apply if the person receiving the income establishes that neither the performer nor any persons related to the performer participate directly or indirectly in the receipts or profits of the person providing the services of the performer. Assume, for example, that a circus owned by a U.S. corporation performs in Sri Lanka, and promoters of the performance in Sri Lanka pay the circus, which, in turn, pays salaries to the circus performers. The circus is determined to have no permanent establishment in Sri Lanka. Since the circus performers do not participate in the profits of the circus, but merely receive their salaries out of the circus' gross receipts, the circus is protected by Article 7 and its income is not subject to host-country tax. Whether the salaries of the circus performers are subject to host-country tax under this Article depends on whether they exceed the $6,000 threshold in paragraph 1.

This exception from paragraph 3 for non-abusive cases is not found in the OECD Model. The United States has entered a reservation to the OECD Model on this point.

Since pursuant to Article 1 (Personal Scope) the Convention only applies to persons who are residents of one of the Contracting States, if the star company is not a resident of one of the Contracting States then taxation of the income is not affected by Article 18 or any other provision of the Convention.

Relationship to other articles

This Article is subject to the provisions of the saving clause of paragraph 3 of Article 1 (Personal Scope). Thus, if an entertainer or a athlete who is resident in Sri Lanka is a citizen of the United States, the United States may tax all of his income from performances in the United States without regard to the provisions of this Article, subject, however, to the special foreign tax credit provisions of Article 24 (Relief from Double Taxation). In addition, benefits of this Article are subject to the provisions of Article 23 (Limitation on Benefits)

Article 19 (Pensions, Social Security and Child Support)

This Article deals with the taxation of private (*i.e.,* non-government service) pensions, social security benefits, and child support payments .

Paragraph 1

Paragraph 1 provides that distributions from pensions and other similar remuneration beneficially owned by a resident of a Contracting State in consideration of past employment are taxable only in the State of residence of the beneficiary. The term "pension distributions and other similar remuneration" includes both periodic and single sum payments.

The phrase "pension distributions and other similar remuneration" is intended to encompass payments made by private retirement plans and arrangements in consideration of past employment. In the United States, the plans encompassed by Paragraph 1 include: qualified plans under section 401(a), individual retirement plans (including individual retirement plans that are part of a simplified employee pension plan that satisfies section

408(k), individual retirement accounts and section 408(p) accounts), section 457(g) governmental plans, section 403(a) qualified annuity plans, and section 403(b) plans. The competent authorities may agree that distributions from other plans that generally meet similar criteria to those applicable to other plans established under their respective laws also qualify for the benefits of Paragraph 1.

Pensions in respect of government service are not covered by this paragraph. They are covered either by paragraph 2 of this Article, if they are in the form of social security benefits, or by Article 20 (Government Service). Thus, Article 20 covers section 457, 401(a) and 403(b) plans established for government employees. If a pension in respect of government service is not covered by Article 20 solely because the service is not "in the discharge of functions of a governmental nature," the pension is covered by this article.

Paragraph 2

Paragraph 2 provides for exclusive source-country taxation of social security benefits. This paragraph provides that, notwithstanding the provision of paragraph 1 under which private pensions are taxable exclusively in the State of residence of the beneficial owner, payments made by one of the Contracting States under the provisions of its social security system to a resident of the other Contracting State will be taxable only in the Contracting State making the payment. This paragraph applies to social security beneficiaries whether they have contributed to the system as private sector or government employees.

Paragraph 3

Paragraph 3 generally covers periodic payments for the support of a minor child made pursuant to a written separation agreement or a decree of divorce, separate maintenance, or compulsory support. Paragraph 3 exempts from tax in both Contracting States such payments made by a resident of a Contracting State to a resident of the other Contracting State. Thus, child support payments from a resident of a Contracting State to a resident of the other Contracting State are taxable in neither Contracting State.

Relationship to other Articles

Paragraph 1 of Article 19 is subject to the saving clause of paragraph 3 of Article 1 (Personal Scope). Thus, a U.S. citizen who is resident in Sri Lanka and receives a U.S. pension will be subject to U.S. net income tax on the payment, notwithstanding the rule in paragraph 1 that gives the State of residence of the recipient the exclusive taxing right.

Paragraphs 2 and 3 of Article 19 are exceptions to the saving clause by virtue of Paragraph 4(a) of Article 1. Accordingly, a U.S. citizen who is a resident of Sri Lanka will not be subject to U.S. tax on any Sri Lanka social security benefits or child support payments.

Article 20 (Government Service)

Article 20 deals with the taxation of government compensation. This Article provides that remuneration paid from the public funds of one of the States or its political subdivisions or its political subdivisions or local authorities to any individual who is rendering services to that State, political subdivision or local authority, which are in the discharge of governmental functions, is exempt from tax by the other State. The paragraph applies both to government employees and to independent contractors engaged by governments to perform services for them.

The remuneration described in this Article is subject to the provisions of this paragraph and not to those of Articles 15 (Independent Personal Services), 16 (Dependent Personal Services), 18 (Artistes and Athletes) or Article 19 (Pensions, Social Security, and Child Support Payments). If, however, the remuneration or pension is paid for services performed in connection with a business carried on the by a Contracting State or a political subdivision or local authority thereof, those other Articles will apply. This provision conforms with the OECD Model.

Relation to other Articles

Under paragraph 4(b) of Article 1 (Personal Scope), the saving clause (paragraph 3 of Article 1) does not apply to the benefits conferred by one of the States under Article 20 if the recipient of the benefits is neither a citizen of that State, nor a person who has been admitted for permanent residence there (*i.e.,* in the United States, a "green card" holder). Thus, a resident of Sri Lanka who, in the course of rendering services to the government of Sri Lanka becomes a resident of the United States (but not a permanent resident), would be entitled to the exemption from source State taxation provided by this Article.

Article 21 (Students and Trainees)

This Article provides regarding the taxation of students, apprentices or business trainees.

Paragraph 1

Paragraph 1 provides that persons who meet the tests of the Article will be exempt from tax with respect to designated classes on income in the State they are visiting (the "host State"). Several conditions must be satisfied in order for an individual to be entitled to the benefits of this Article.

First, the visitor must have been, either at the time of his arrival in the host State or immediately before, a resident of the other Contracting State.
Second, the purpose of the visit must be the full-time education or training of the visitor. Thus, if the visitor comes principally to work in the host State but also is a part-time student, he would not be entitled to the benefits of this Article, even with respect to

any payments he may receive from abroad for his maintenance or education, and regardless of whether or not he is in a degree program. Whether a student is to be considered full-time will be determined by the rules of the educational institution where he is studying. A person who visits the host State to obtain business training and who also receives a salary from his employer for providing services would not be considered a trainee and would not be entitled to the benefits of this Article with respect to the payments for services.

The host-country exemption in Article 21 applies only to payments arising outside the host State that are received by the student, apprentice or business trainee for the purpose of his maintenance, education or training. A payment will be considered to arise outside the host State if the payer is located outside the host State. Thus, if an employer from one of the Contracting States sends an employee to the other Contracting State for training, the payments the trainee receives from abroad from his employer for his maintenance or training while he is present in the host State will be exempt from host-country tax. Where appropriate, substance prevails over form in determining the identity of the payer. Thus, for example, payments made directly or indirectly by the U.S. person with whom the visitor is training, but which have been routed through a source outside the United States (*e.g.,* a foreign bank account) are not treated as arising outside the United States for this purpose.

Paragraph 2

Under paragraph 2, an individual who is a resident of one Contracting State at the time he becomes temporarily present in the other Contracting State and who is temporarily present therein as an employee of, or under contract with, a resident of the first-mentioned Contracting State, for the primary purpose of acquiring technical, professional, or business experience from a person other than that resident of the first-mentioned Contracting State or other than a person related to such resident, or studying at a university or other recognized educational institution in that other Contracting State, will be exempt from tax by that other Contracting State for a period of twelve consecutive months, on income from personal services not in excess of $6,000 or its equivalent in Sri Lankan rupees.

The saving clause of paragraph 3 of Article 1 (Personal Scope) does not apply to this Article with respect to an individual who is neither a citizen of the host State nor has been admitted for permanent residence there. The saving clause, however, does apply with respect to citizens and permanent residents of the host State. Accordingly, a U.S. citizen who is a resident of Sri Lanka and who visits the United States as a full-time student will not be exempt from U.S. tax on remittances from abroad that otherwise constitute U.S. taxable income. Under subparagraph (b) of paragraph 4 of Article 1, however, a Sri Lankan resident who is not a U.S. citizen, and who visits the United States as a student and remains long enough to become a resident under U.S. law, but does not become a permanent resident (*i.e.,* does not acquire a green card), will be entitled to the full benefits of the Article.

Article 22 (Other Income)

Article 22 generally assigns taxing jurisdiction over income not dealt with in the other articles (Articles 6 through 21) of the Convention. An item of income is "dealt with" in another article if it is the type of income described in the article and it has its source in a Contracting State. For example, all royalty income that arises in a Contracting State and that is beneficially owned by a resident of the other Contracting State is "dealt with" in Article 12 (Royalties).

Examples of items of income covered by Article 22 include income from gambling, punitive (but not compensatory) damages, covenants not to compete, and income from certain financial instruments to the extent derived by persons not engaged in the trade or business of dealing in such instruments (unless the transaction giving rise to the income is related to a trade or business, in which case it is dealt with under Article 7 (Business Profits)). The article also applies to items of income that are not dealt with in the other articles because of their source or some other characteristic. For example, Article 11 (Interest) addresses only the taxation of interest arising in a Contracting State. Interest arising in a third State that is not attributable to a permanent establishment, therefore, is subject to Article 22.

Distributions from partnerships and trust distributions are not generally dealt with under Article 22 because partnership distributions generally do not constitute income. Under the Code, partners include in income their distributive share of partnership income annually, and partnership distributions themselves generally do not give rise to income. This would also be the case under U.S. law with respect to distributions from trusts. Under the Code, the trust income and distributions have the character of the associated distributable net income and therefore would generally be covered by another article of the Convention. See Code section 641 et seq.

Paragraph 1

The general rule of Article 22 is contained in paragraph 1. Subject to paragraph 2, items of income not dealt with in other articles and beneficially owned by a resident of a Contracting State will be taxable only in the State of residence. This exclusive right of taxation applies whether or not the residence State exercises its right to tax the income covered by the Article.

Paragraph 2

Paragraph 2 modifies the exclusive residence State taxation right to tax "other income" granted by paragraph 1. Under this paragraph, "other income" which arises in a Contracting State may be taxed by that State even if it is received by a resident of the other Contracting State. This is not an exclusive taxing right; the residence State may continue to tax. Any resulting double taxation is taken care of by the provisions of Article 24 (Relief from Double Taxation). This rule is taken from the U.N. Model, and is consistent with the rules of several other U.S. treaties.

Article 23 (Limitation on Benefits)

Purpose of Limitation on Benefits Provisions

The United States views an income tax treaty as a vehicle for providing treaty benefits to residents of the two Contracting States. The proper operation of a treaty requires that it apply to those that are <u>bona fide</u> residents of one of the Contracting States for the purpose of being granted treaty benefits. This principal has long been recognized. For example, the Commentaries to the OECD Model authorize a tax authority to deny treaty benefits, under substance-over-form principles, to a nominee in one State deriving income from the other on behalf of a third-country resident. In addition, although the text of the OECD Model does not contain express anti-abuse provisions, the Commentary to Article 1 contains an extensive discussion regarding the appropriateness of such provisions in tax treaties in order to limit the ability of third state residents to obtain treaty benefits. The United States holds strongly to the view that tax treaties should include provisions that specifically prevent misuse of treaties by residents of third countries. Consequently, all recent U.S. income tax treaties contain comprehensive Limitation on Benefits provisions.

A treaty that provides treaty benefits to any resident of a Contracting State permits "treaty shopping": the use, by residents of third states, of legal entities established in a Contracting State with a principal purpose to obtain the benefits of a tax treaty between the United States and the other Contracting State. Treaty shopping does not encompass every case in which a third state resident establishes an entity in a U.S. treaty partner, and that entity enjoys treaty benefits to which the third state resident would not itself be entitled. If the third country resident had substantial reasons for establishing the structure that were unrelated to obtaining treaty benefits, the use of the entity in the U.S. treaty partner structure would not fall within this concept of treaty shopping.

An anti-treaty shopping approach that required the tax authority to investigate the taxpayer's motives in establishing an entity in a particular country would be difficult to administer. In order to avoid the necessity of making such a subjective determination, Article 23 sets forth a series of objective tests. The assumption underlying each of these tests is that a taxpayer that satisfies the requirements of the test likely has a real business purpose for the structure it has adopted, or has a sufficiently strong nexus to the other Contracting State (*e.g.,* a resident individual) to warrant benefits even in the absence of a business connection, and that this business purpose or connection is sufficient to justify the conclusion that obtaining the benefits of the treaty is not a principal purpose of establishing or maintaining residence in that other State.

For instance, the assumption underlying the active trade or business test under paragraph 3 is that a third country resident that establishes a "substantial" operation in Sri Lanka and that derives income from a similar activity in the United States would not do so primarily to avail itself of the benefits of the Convention; it is presumed in such a case that the investor had a valid business purpose for investing in Sri Lanka, and that the link between that trade or business and the U.S. activity that generates the treaty-benefited income manifests a business purpose for placing the U.S. investments in the entity in Sri Lanka. It is considered unlikely that the investor would incur the expense of establishing a substantial trade or business in Sri Lanka simply to obtain the benefits of the Convention. A similar rationale underlies the other tests in Article 23.

While these tests provide useful surrogates for identifying actual intent, these mechanical tests cannot account for every case in which the taxpayer was not treaty shopping. Accordingly, Article 23 also includes a provision (paragraph 4) authorizing the competent authority of a Contracting State to grant benefits in situations where none of the other tests of Article 23 is met. While an analysis under paragraph 4 may well differ from that under one of the other tests of Article 23, its objective is the same: to identify investors whose residence in the other State can be justified by factors other than a purpose to derive treaty benefits.

Article 23 and the anti-abuse provisions of domestic law complement each other, as Article 23 effectively determines whether an entity has a sufficient nexus to the Contracting State to be treated as a resident for treaty purposes, while domestic anti-abuse provisions (*e.g.,* business purpose, substance-over-form, step transaction or conduit principles) determine whether a particular transaction should be recast in accordance with its substance. Thus, internal law principles of the source State may be applied to identify the beneficial owner of an item of income, and Article 23 then will be applied to the beneficial owner to determine if that person is entitled to the benefits of the Convention with respect to such income.

Structure of the Article

Article 23 follows the form used in other recent U.S. income tax treaties. Paragraph 1 states the general rule that a resident of a Contracting State is entitled to benefits otherwise accorded to residents only to the extent provided in the Article. Paragraph 2 lists a series of attributes of a resident of a Contracting State, the presence of any one of which will entitle that person to all the benefits of the Convention. Paragraph 3 provides that, with respect to a person not entitled to benefits under paragraph 2, benefits nonetheless may be granted to that person with regard to certain types of income. Paragraph 4 provides that benefits also may be granted if the competent authority of the State from which benefits are claimed determines that it is appropriate to provide benefits in that case. Paragraph 5 defines the term "recognized stock exchange" as used in paragraph 2(c).

Paragraph 1

Paragraph 1 provides that a resident of a Contracting State will be entitled to the benefits otherwise accorded to residents of a Contracting State under the Convention only to the extent provided in the Article. The benefits otherwise accorded to residents under the Convention include all limitations on source-based taxation under Articles 6 through 22, the treaty-based relief from double taxation provided by Article 24 (Relief from Double Taxation), and the protection afforded to residents of a Contracting State under

Article 25 (Nondiscrimination). Some provisions do not require that a person be a resident in order to enjoy the benefits of those provisions. These include paragraph 1 of Article 25 (Non- Discrimination), Article 26 (Mutual Agreement Procedure), and Article 28 (Diplomatic Agents and Consular Officers). Article 23 accordingly does not limit the availability of the benefits of these provisions.

Paragraph 2

Paragraph 2 has six subparagraphs, each of which describes a category of residents that are entitled to all benefits of the Convention.

Individuals -- Subparagraph 2(a)

Subparagraph (a) provides that individual residents of a Contracting State will be entitled to all treaty benefits. If such an individual receives income as a nominee on behalf of a third country resident, benefits may be denied under the respective articles of the Convention by the requirement that the beneficial owner of the income be a resident of a Contracting State.

Qualified Governmental Entities -- Subparagraph 2(b)

Subparagraph (b) provides that qualified governmental entities, as defined in subparagraph 3(j) of Article 3 (Definitions), also will be entitled to all benefits of the Convention. As described in Article 3, in addition to federal, state and local governments, the term "qualified governmental entity" encompasses certain government-owned corporations and other entities, and certain pension trusts or funds that administer pension benefits described in Article 19 (Government Service).

Publicly-Traded Corporations -- Subparagraph 2(c)(i)

Subparagraph (c) applies to two categories of corporations: publicly-traded corporations and subsidiaries of publicly-traded corporations. Clause (i) of subparagraph 2(c) provides that a company will be entitled to all the benefits of the Convention if all the shares in the class or classes of shares that represent more than 50 percent of the voting power and value of the company are regularly traded on a "recognized stock exchange" located in either State. The term "recognized stock exchange" is defined in paragraph 5.

If a company has only one class of shares, it is only necessary to consider whether the shares of that class are regularly traded on a recognized stock exchange. If the company has more than one class of shares, it is necessary as an initial matter to determine whether one of the classes accounts for more than half of the voting power and value of the company. If so, then only those shares are considered for purposes of the regular trading requirement. If no single class of shares accounts for more than half of the company's voting power and value, it is necessary to identify a group of two or more classes of the company's shares that account for more than half of the company's voting power and value, and then to determine whether each class of shares in this group satisfies the regular trading requirement. Although in a particular case involving a company with several classes of shares it is conceivable that more than one group of classes could be identified that account for more than 50% of the shares, it is only necessary for one such group to satisfy the requirements of this subparagraph in order for the company to be entitled to benefits. Benefits would not be denied to the company even if a second, non-qualifying, group of shares with more than half of the company's voting power and value could be identified.

The term "regularly traded" is not defined in the Convention. In accordance with paragraph 2 of Article 3 (General Definitions), this term will be defined by reference to the domestic tax laws of the State from which treaty benefits are sought (i.e., the source State). In the case of the United States, this term is understood to have the meaning it has under Treas. Reg. section 1.884-5(d)(4)(i)(B), relating to the branch tax provisions of the Code. Under these regulations, a class of shares is considered to be "regularly traded" if two requirements are met: trades in the class of shares are made in more than de minimis quantities on at least 60 days during the taxable year, and the aggregate number of shares in the class traded during the year is at least 10 percent of the average number of shares outstanding during the year. Sections 1.884-5(d)(4)(i)(A), (ii) and (iii) will not be taken into account for purposes of defining the term "regularly traded" under the Convention.

The regular trading requirement can be met by trading on any recognized exchange or exchanges located in either State. Trading on one or more recognized stock exchanges may be aggregated for purposes of this requirement. Thus, a U.S. company could satisfy the regularly traded requirement through trading, in whole or in part, on a recognized stock exchange located in the other Contracting State. Authorized but unissued shares are not considered for purposes of this test.

<u>Subsidiaries of Publicly-Traded Corporations -- Subparagraph 2(c)(ii)</u>

Clause (ii) of subparagraph 2(c) provides a test under which certain companies that are directly or indirectly controlled by companies satisfying the publicly-traded test of subparagraph 2(c)(i) may be entitled to the benefits of the Convention. Under this test, a company will be entitled to the benefits of the Convention if 50 percent or more of each class of shares in the company is directly or indirectly owned by companies that are described in subparagraph 2(c)(i).

This test differs from that under subparagraph 2(c)(i) in that 50 percent of each class of the company's shares, not merely the class or classes accounting for more than 50 percent of the company's votes and value, must be held by publicly-traded companies described in subparagraph 2(c)(i). Thus, the test under subparagraph 2(c)(i) considers the ownership of every class of shares outstanding, while the test under subparagraph 2(c)(ii) only considers those classes that account for a majority of the company's voting power and value.

Clause (ii) permits indirect ownership. Consequently, the ownership by publicly-traded companies described in clause (i) need not be direct. However, any intermediate owners in the chain of ownership must themselves be entitled to benefits under paragraph 2.

Tax Exempt Organizations -- Subparagraph 2(d)

Subparagraph 2(d) provides that the tax exempt organizations described in subparagraph 1(c)(i) of Article 4 (Resident) will be entitled to all the benefits of the Convention. These entities are entities that generally are exempt from tax in their State of residence and that are organized and operated exclusively to fulfill religious, educational, scientific and other charitable purposes. Unlike some recent U.S. treaties, there is no requirement that specified percentages of the beneficiaries of these organizations be residents of one of the Contracting States.

Pension Funds -- Subparagraph 2(e)

Subparagraph 2(e) provides that organizations described in subparagraph 1(c)(ii) of Article 4 (Resident) will be entitled to all the benefits of the Convention, as long as more than half of the beneficiaries, members or participants of the organization are individual residents of either Contracting State. The organizations referred to in this provision are tax-exempt entities that provide pension and other benefits to employees pursuant to a plan. For purposes of this provision, the term "beneficiaries" should be understood to refer to the persons receiving benefits from the organization.

Ownership/Base Erosion -- Subparagraph 2(f)

Subparagraph 2(f) provides an additional test that applies to any form of legal entity that is a resident of a Contracting State. The test provided in paragraph (f), the so-called ownership, base erosion test, is a two-part test. Both prongs of the test must be satisfied for the resident to be entitled to benefits under subparagraph 2(f).

The ownership prong of the test, under clause (i), requires that 50 percent or more of each class of beneficial interests in the person (in the case of a corporation, 50 percent or more of each class of its shares) be owned on at least half the days of the person's taxable year by persons who are themselves entitled to benefits under the other tests of paragraph 2 (*i.e.,* subparagraphs (a), (b), (c), (d), or (e)). The ownership may be indirect through other persons themselves entitled to benefits under paragraph 2.

Trusts may be entitled to benefits under this provision if they are treated as residents under Article 4 (Resident) and they otherwise satisfy the requirements of this subparagraph. For purposes of this subparagraph, the beneficial interests in a trust will be considered to be owned by its beneficiaries in proportion to each beneficiary's actuarial interest in the trust. The interest of a remainder beneficiary will be equal to 100 percent less the aggregate percentages held by income beneficiaries. A beneficiary's interest in a trust will not be considered to be owned by a person entitled to benefits under the other provisions of paragraph 2 if it is not possible to determine the beneficiary's actuarial interest. Consequently, if it is not possible to determine the actuarial interest of any beneficiaries in a trust, the ownership test under clause (i) cannot be satisfied, unless all possible beneficiaries are persons entitled to benefits under the other subparagraphs of paragraph 2.

The base erosion prong of clause (ii) of subparagraph (f) disqualifies a person if fifty percent or more of the person's gross income for the taxable year be paid or accrued, directly or indirectly, to a person or persons who are not residents of either Contracting State (unless income is attributable to a permanent establishment located in either Contracting State), in the form of payments deductible for tax purposes in the payer's State of residence.

To the extent they are deductible from the taxable base, trust distributions are deductible payments. However, depreciation and amortization deductions, which do not represent payments or accruals to other persons, are disregarded for this purpose. Deductible payments also do not include arm's length payments in the ordinary course of business for services or tangible property or with respect to financial obligations to banks that are residents of either Contracting State, or that have a permanent establishment in either Contracting State to which the payment is attributable.

The term "gross income" is not defined in the Convention. Thus, in accordance with paragraph 2 of Article 3 (General Definitions), in determining whether a person deriving income from United States sources is entitled to the benefits of the Convention, the United States will ascribe the meaning to the term that it has in the United States. In such cases, "gross income" will be defined as gross receipts less cost of goods sold.

It is intended that the provisions of paragraph 2 will be self executing. Unlike the provisions of paragraph 4, discussed below, claiming benefits under paragraph 2 does not require advance competent authority ruling or approval. The tax authorities may, of course, on review, determine that the taxpayer has improperly interpreted the paragraph and is not entitled to the benefits claimed.

Paragraph 3

Paragraph 3 sets forth a test under which a resident of a Contracting State that is not generally entitled to benefits of the Convention under paragraph 2 may receive treaty benefits with respect to certain items of income that are connected to an active trade or business conducted in its State of residence.

Subparagraph (a) sets forth a three-pronged test that must be satisfied in order for a resident of a Contracting State to be entitled to the benefits of the Convention with respect to a particular item of income. First, the resident must be engaged in the active conduct of a trade of business in its State of residence. Second, the income derived from the other State must be derived in connection with, or be incidental to, that trade or business. Third, the trade or business must be substantial in relation to the activity in the other State that generated the item of income.

Trade or Business -- Subparagraphs 3(a)(i) and (b)

The term "trade or business" is not defined in the Convention. Pursuant to paragraph 2 of Article 3 (General Definitions), when determining whether a resident of Sri Lanka is entitled to the benefits of the Convention under paragraph 3 of this Article with respect to an item of income derived from sources within the United States, the United States will ascribe to this term the meaning that it has under the law of the United States. Accordingly, the U.S. competent authority will refer to the regulations issued under section 367(a) for the definition of the term "trade or business." In general, therefore, a trade or business will be considered to be a specific unified group of activities that constitute or could constitute an independent economic enterprise carried on for profit. Furthermore, a corporation generally will be considered to carry on a trade or business only if the officers and employees of the corporation conduct substantial managerial and operational activities.

Notwithstanding this general definition of trade or business, subparagraph 3(b) provides that the business of making or managing investments for the resident's own account will be considered to be a trade or business only when part of banking, insurance or securities activities conducted by a bank, insurance company, or registered securities dealer. Such activities conducted by a person other than a bank, insurance company or registered securities dealer will not be considered to be the conduct of an active trade or business, nor would they be considered to be the conduct of an active trade or business if conducted by a bank, insurance company or registered securities dealer but not as part of the company's banking, insurance or dealer business.

Because a headquarters operation is in the business of managing investments, a company that functions solely as a headquarter company will not be considered to be engaged in an active trade or business for purposes of paragraph 3(a).

Derived in Connection With Requirement -- Subparagraphs 3(a)(ii) and (d)

Subparagraph 3(d) provides that income is derived in connection with a trade or business if the income-producing activity in the State of source is a line of business that forms a part of or is complementary to the trade or business conducted in the State of residence by the income recipient. A business activity generally will be considered to "form a part of" a business activity conducted in the State of source if the two activities involve the design, manufacture or sale of the same products or type of products, or the provision of similar services.

EXAMPLE 1. USCo is a corporation resident in the United States. USCo is engaged in an active manufacturing business in the United States. USCo owns 100 percent of the shares of SLCo, a corporation resident in Sri Lanka. SLCo distributes USCo products in Sri Lanka. Because the business activities conducted by the two corporations involve the same products, SLCo's distribution business is considered to form a part of USCo's manufacturing.

EXAMPLE 2. The facts are the same as in Example 1, except that USCo does not manufacture. Rather, USCo operates a large research and development facility in the United States that licenses intellectual property to affiliates worldwide, including SLCo. SLCo and other USCo affiliates then manufacture and market the USCo-designed products in their respective markets. Since the activities conducted by SLCo and USCo involve the same product lines, these activities are considered to form a part of the same trade or business.

For two activities to be considered to be "complementary," the activities need not relate to the same types of products or services, but they should be part of the same overall industry and be related in the sense that the success or failure of one activity will tend to result in success or failure for the other. Where more than one trade or business is conducted in the State of source and only one of the trades or businesses forms a part of or is complementary to a trade or business conducted in the State of residence, it is necessary to identify the trade or business to which an item of income is attributable. Royalties generally will be considered to be derived in connection with the trade or business to which the underlying intangible property is attributable. Dividends will be deemed to be derived first out of earnings and profits of the treaty-benefited trade or business, and then out of other earnings and profits. Interest income may be allocated under any reasonable method consistently applied. A method that conforms to U.S. principles for expense allocation will be considered a reasonable method.

EXAMPLE 3. Americair is a corporation resident in the United States that operates an international airline. SLSub is a wholly-owned subsidiary of Americair resident in Sri Lanka. SLSub operates a chain of hotels in Sri Lanka that are located near airports served by Americair flights. Americair frequently sells tour packages that include air travel to Sri Lanka and lodging at SLSub hotels. Although both companies are engaged in the active conduct of a trade or business, the businesses of operating a chain of hotels and operating an airline are distinct trades or businesses. Therefore SLSub's business does not form a part of Americair's business. However, SLSub's business is considered to be complementary to Americair's business because they are part of the same overall industry (travel) and the links between their operations tend to make them interdependent.

EXAMPLE 4. The facts are the same as in Example 3, except that SLSub owns an office building in Sri Lanka instead of a hotel chain. No part of Americair's business is conducted through the office building. SLSub's business is not considered to form a part of or to be complementary to Americair's business. They are engaged in distinct trades or businesses in separate industries, and there is no economic dependence between the two operations.

EXAMPLE 5. USFlower is a corporation resident in the United States. USFlower produces and sells flowers in the United States and other countries. USFlower owns all the shares of SLHolding, a corporation resident in Sri Lanka. SLHolding is a holding company that is not engaged in a trade or business. SLHolding owns all the shares of three corporations that are resident in Sri Lanka: SLFlower, SLLawn, and SLFish. SLFlower distributes USFlower flowers under the USFlower trademark in Sri Lanka. SLLawn markets a line of lawn care products in Sri Lanka under the USFlower trademark. In addition to being sold under the same trademark, SLLawn and SLFlower products are sold in the same stores and sales of each company's products tend to generate increased sales of the other's products. SLFish imports fish from the United States and distributes it to fish wholesalers in Sri Lanka. For purposes of paragraph 3, the business of SLFlower forms a part of the business of USFlower, the business of SLLawn is complementary to the business of USFlower, and the business of SLFish is neither part of nor complementary to that of USFlower.

Finally, a resident in one of the States also will be entitled to the benefits of the Convention with respect to income derived from the other State if the income is "incidental" to the trade or business conducted in the recipient's State of residence. Subparagraph 3(d) provides that income derived from a State will be incidental to a trade or business conducted in the other State if the production of such income facilitates the conduct of the trade or business in the other State. An example of incidental income is the temporary investment of working capital derived from a trade or business.

Substantiality -- Subparagraphs 3(a)(iii) and (c)

As indicated above, subparagraph 3(a)(iii) provides that income that a resident of a State derives from the other State will be entitled to the benefits of the Convention under paragraph 3 only if the income is derived in connection with a trade or business conducted in the recipient's State of residence and that trade or business is "substantial" in relation to the income-producing activity in the State of source. Subparagraph 3(c) provides that whether the trade or business of the income recipient is substantial will be determined based on all the facts and circumstances. These circumstances generally would include comparative sizes of the trades or businesses in each Contracting State (measured by reference to asset values, income and payroll expenses), the nature of the activities performed in each Contracting State, and the relative contributions made to that trade or business in each Contracting State. In making each determination or comparison, due regard will be given to the relative sizes of the U.S. and Sri Lankan economies.

The determination in subparagraph 3(a)(iii) also is made separately for each item of income derived from the State of source. It therefore is possible that a person would be entitled to the benefits of the Convention with respect to one item of income but not with respect to another. If a resident of a Contracting State is entitled to treaty benefits with respect to a particular item of income under paragraph 3, the resident is entitled to all benefits of the Convention insofar as they affect the taxation of that item of income.

The substantiality requirement is intended to prevent a narrow case of treaty-shopping abuse in which a company attempts to qualify for benefits by engaging in de minimis connected business activities in the treaty country in which it is resident (*i.e.*, activities that have little economic cost or effect with respect to the company business as a whole).

In addition to the subjective rule, subparagraph 3(c) provides a safe harbor under which the trade or business of the income recipient may be deemed to be substantial based on three ratios that compare the size of the recipient's activities to those conducted in the other State. The three ratios compare: (i) the value of the assets in the recipient's State to the assets used in the other State; (ii) the gross income derived in the recipient's State to the gross income derived in the other State; and (iii) the payroll expense in the recipient's State to the payroll expense in the other State. The average of the three ratios with respect to the preceding taxable year must exceed 10 percent, and each individual ratio must exceed 7.5 percent. If any individual ratio does not exceed 7.5 percent for the preceding taxable year, the average for the three preceding taxable years may be used instead. Thus, if the taxable year is 2005, the preceding year is 2004. If one of the ratios for 2004 is not greater than 7.5 percent, the average ratio for 2002, 2003, and 2004 with respect to that item may be used.

The term "value" also is not defined in the Convention. Therefore, this term also will be defined under U.S. law for purposes of determining whether a person deriving income from United States sources is entitled to the benefits of the Convention. In such cases, "value" generally will be defined using the method used by the taxpayer in keeping its books for purposes of financial reporting in its country of residence. See Treas. Reg. section 1.884-5(e)(3)(ii)(A).

Only items actually located or incurred in the two Contracting States are included in the computation of the ratios. If the person from whom the income in the other State is derived is not wholly-owned by the recipient (and parties related thereto) then the items included in the computation with respect to such person must be reduced by a percentage equal to the percentage control held by persons not related to the recipient. For instance, if a United States corporation derives income from a corporation in the other State in which it holds 80 percent of the shares, and unrelated parties hold the remaining shares, for purposes of subparagraph 3(c) only 80 percent of the assets, payroll and gross income of the company in the other State would be taken into account.

Consequently, if neither the recipient nor a person related to the recipient has an ownership interest in the person from whom the income is derived, the substantiality test always will be satisfied (the denominator in the computation of each ratio will be zero and the numerator will be a positive number). Of course, the other two prongs of the test under paragraph 3 would have to be satisfied in order for the recipient of the item of income to receive treaty benefits with respect to that income. For example, assume that a resident of a Contracting State is in the business of banking in that State. The bank loans money to unrelated residents of the United States. The bank would satisfy the substantiality requirement of this subparagraph with respect to interest paid on the loans because it has no ownership interest in the payers.

Paragraph 4

Paragraph 4 provides that a resident of one of the States that is not otherwise entitled to the benefits of the Convention may be granted benefits under the Convention if the competent authority of the State from which benefits are claimed so determines. This discretionary provision is included in recognition of the fact that, with the increasing scope and diversity of international economic relations, there may be cases where significant participation by third country residents in an enterprise of a Contracting State is warranted by sound business practice or long-standing business structures and does not necessarily indicate a motive of attempting to derive unintended Convention benefits.

The competent authority of a State will base a determination under this paragraph on whether the establishment, acquisition, or maintenance of the person seeking benefits under the Convention, or the conduct of such person's operations, has or had as one of its principal purposes the obtaining of benefits under the Convention. Thus, persons that establish operations in one of the States with the principal purpose of obtaining the benefits of the Convention ordinarily will not be granted relief under paragraph 4.

The competent authority may determine to grant all benefits of the Convention, or it may determine to grant only certain benefits. For instance, it may determine to grant benefits only with respect to a particular item of income in a manner similar to paragraph 3. Further, the competent authority may set time limits on the duration of any relief granted.

It is assumed that, for purposes of implementing paragraph 4, a taxpayer will not be required to wait until the tax authorities of one of the States have determined that benefits are denied before he will be permitted to seek a determination under this paragraph. In these circumstances, it is also expected that if the competent authority determines that benefits are to be allowed, they will be allowed retroactively to the time of entry into force of the relevant treaty provision or the establishment of the structure in question, whichever is later.

Finally, there may be cases in which a resident of a Contracting State may apply for discretionary relief to the competent authority of his State of residence. For instance, a resident of a State could apply to the competent authority of his State of residence in a case in which he had been denied a treaty-based credit under Article 24 (Relief from Double Taxation) on the grounds that he was not entitled to benefits of the article under Article 23.

Paragraph 5

Paragraph 5 provides that the term "recognized stock exchange" means (i) the NASDAQ System owned by the National Association of Securities Dealers, and any stock exchange registered with the Securities and Exchange Commission as a national securities exchange for purposes of the Securities Exchange Act of 1934; (ii) the Colombo Stock Exchange; and (3) any other stock exchange agreed upon by the competent authorities of the Contracting States.

Article 24 (Relief From Double Taxation)

This Article describes the manner in which each Contracting State undertakes to relieve double taxation. The United States uses the foreign tax credit method under its internal law, and by treaty.

Paragraph 1

The United States agrees, in paragraph 1, to allow to its citizens and residents a credit against U.S. tax for the appropriate amount of income taxes paid or accrued to Sri Lanka. Paragraph 1 also provides for a deemed-paid credit, consistent with section 902 of the Code, to a U.S. corporation in respect of dividends received from a corporation resident in Sri Lanka of which the U.S. corporation owns at least 10 percent of the voting stock. This credit is for the tax paid by the corporation of Sri Lanka on the profits out of which the dividends are considered paid. For purposes of paragraph 1, the taxes covered by subparagraph (a) of paragraph 2 and by paragraph 3 of Article 2 (Covered Taxes) are Sri Lankan taxes.

The credits allowed under paragraph 1 are allowed in accordance with the provisions and subject to the limitations of U.S. law, as that law may be amended over time, so long as the general principle of this Article, i.e., the allowance of a credit, is retained. Thus, although the Convention provides for a foreign tax credit, the terms of the credit are determined by the provisions, at the time a credit is given, of the U.S. statutory credit.

Therefore, the U.S. credit under the Convention is subject to the various limitations of U.S. law (see Code sections 901 - 908). For example, the credit against U.S. tax generally is limited to the amount of U.S. tax due with respect to net foreign source income within the relevant foreign tax credit limitation category (see Code section 904(a) and (d)), and the dollar amount of the credit is determined in accordance with U.S. currency translation rules (see, e.g., Code section 986). Similarly, U.S. law applies to determine carryover periods for excess credits and other inter-year adjustments. When the alternative minimum tax is due, the alternative minimum tax foreign tax credit generally is limited in accordance with U.S. law to 90 percent of alternative minimum tax liability.

Paragraph 2

Paragraph 2 provides that taxes paid to Sri Lanka by a company which is a resident of Sri Lanka on a distribution or remittance of dividends will be regarded as a tax on the shareholder for purposes of the credit allowed by the United States.

Paragraph 3

Sri Lanka agrees, in paragraph 3, to allow to its residents a credit against the Sri Lanka tax for the appropriate amount of income taxes paid or accrued to the United States. Paragraph 3 also provides for a deemed-paid credit to a Sri Lankan corporation in respect of dividends received from a corporation resident in United States of which the Sri Lankan corporation owns at least 10 percent of the voting stock. This credit is for the tax paid by the corporation of the United States on the profits out of which the dividends are considered paid. For purposes of paragraph 3, the taxes covered by subparagraph (b) of paragraph 2 and by paragraph 3 of Article 2 (Covered Taxes) are U.S. taxes.

Paragraph 4

Paragraph 4 provides that, for purposes of this Article, income which may be taxed in a Contracting State under the terms of this Convention will be considered to have its source in that State. However, domestic law source rules that apply for purposes of limiting the foreign tax credit will govern if they differ from the rules resulting from the treaty source rules. This permits the United States to apply the anti-abuse rules of Code section 904(g), for example.

Article 25 (Nondiscrimination)

This Article assures that nationals of a Contracting State, in the case of paragraph 1, and residents of a Contracting State, in the case of paragraphs 2 through 4, will not be subject, directly or indirectly, to discriminatory taxation in the other Contracting State. For this purpose, non-discrimination means providing national treatment. Not all differences in tax treatment, either as between nationals of the two States, or between residents of the two States, are violations of this national treatment standard. Rather, the national treatment obligation of this Article applies only if the nationals or residents of the two States are comparably situated.

Each of the relevant paragraphs of the Article provides that two persons that are comparably situated must be treated similarly. Although the actual words differ from paragraph to paragraph (e.g., paragraph 1 refers to two nationals "in the same circumstances," paragraph 2 refers to two enterprises "carrying on the same activities" and paragraph 4 refers to two enterprises that are "similar"), the common underlying premise is that if the difference in treatment is directly related to a tax-relevant difference in the situations of the domestic and foreign persons being compared, that difference is not to be treated as discriminatory (e.g., if one person is taxable in a Contracting State on worldwide income and the other is not, or tax may be collectible from one person at a later stage, but not from the other, distinctions in treatment would be justified under paragraph 1). Other examples of such factors that can lead to non-discriminatory differences in treatment will be noted in the discussions of each paragraph.

The operative paragraphs of the Article also use different language to identify the kinds of differences in taxation treatment that will be considered discriminatory. For example, paragraphs 1 and 4 speak of "any taxation or any requirement connected therewith that is other or more burdensome," while paragraph 2 specifies that a tax "shall not be less favorably levied." Regardless of these differences in language, only differences in tax treatment that materially disadvantage the foreign person relative to the domestic person are properly the subject of the Article.

Paragraph 1 provides that a national of one Contracting State may not be subject to taxation or connected requirements in the other Contracting State that are other than or more burdensome than the taxes and connected requirements imposed upon a national of that other State in the same circumstances. As noted above, whether or not the two persons are both taxable on worldwide income is a significant circumstance for this purpose. The use of the term "other" in paragraph 1 does not simply refer to different requirements; the only relevant question under this provision should be whether the requirement imposed on a national of the other State is more burdensome. A requirement may be different from the requirements imposed on U.S. nationals without being more burdensome.

A national of a Contracting State is afforded protection under paragraph 1 even if the national is not a resident of either Contracting State. Accordingly, a U.S. citizen who is resident in a third country is entitled, under this paragraph, to the same treatment in Sri Lanka as a national of Sri Lanka who is in similar circumstances (i.e., presumably one who is resident in a third State). The term "national" in relation to a Contracting State is defined in subparagraph 1(h) of Article 3 (General Definitions).

Because the relevant circumstances referred to in the paragraph relate, among other things, to taxation on worldwide income, the Convention specifically provides that a U.S. national who is not a resident in the United States is not in the same circumstances as a Sri Lanka national who is not a resident of the United States. United States citizens who are not residents of the United States but who are, nevertheless, subject to United States tax on their worldwide income are not in the same circumstances with respect to United States taxation as citizens of the other Contracting State who are not United States residents. Thus, for example, Article 25 would not entitle a national of the other Contracting State resident in a third country to taxation at graduated rates of U.S. source dividends or other investment income that applies to a U.S. citizen resident in the same third country.

Paragraph 2

Paragraph 2 of the Article, like the comparable paragraphs in the OECD and U.S. Models, provides that a Contracting State may not tax a permanent establishment of an enterprise of the other Contracting State less favorably than an enterprise of that first-mentioned State that is carrying on the same activities. This provision, however, does not obligate a Contracting State to grant to a resident of the other Contracting State any tax allowances, reliefs, etc., that it grants to its own residents on account of their civil status or family responsibilities. Thus, if a sole proprietor who is a resident of Sri Lanka has a permanent establishment in the United States, in assessing income tax on the profits attributable to the permanent establishment, the United States is not obligated to allow to the resident of Sri Lanka the personal allowances for himself and his family that he would be permitted to take if the permanent establishment were a sole proprietorship owned and operated by a U.S. resident, despite the fact that the individual income tax rates would apply.

The fact that a U.S. permanent establishment of an enterprise of Sri Lanka is subject to U.S. tax only on income that is attributable to the permanent establishment, while a U.S. corporation engaged in the same activities is taxable on its worldwide income is not, in itself, a sufficient difference to deny national treatment to the permanent establishment. There are cases, however, where the two enterprises would not be similarly situated and differences in treatment may be warranted. For instance, it would not be a violation of the non-discrimination protection of paragraph 2 to require the foreign enterprise to provide information in a reasonable manner that may be different from the information requirements imposed on a resident enterprise, because information may not be as readily available to the Internal Revenue Service from a foreign as from a domestic enterprise. Similarly, it would not be a violation of paragraph 2 to impose penalties on persons who fail to comply with such a requirement (see. e.g., sections 874(a) and 882(c)(2)). Further, a determination that income and expenses have been attributed or allocated to a permanent establishment in conformity with the principles of Article 7 (Business Profits) implies that the attribution or allocation was not discriminatory.

Section 1446 of the Code imposes on any partnership with income that is effectively connected with a U.S. trade or business the obligation to withhold tax on amounts allocable to a foreign partner. In the context of the Convention, this obligation applies with respect to a share of the partnership income of a partner resident in Sri Lanka, and attributable to a U.S. permanent establishment. There is no similar obligation with respect to the distributive shares of U.S. resident partners. It is understood, however, that this distinction is not a form of discrimination within the meaning of paragraph 2 of the Article. No distinction is made between U.S. and non-U.S. partnerships, since the law requires that partnerships of both U.S. and non-U.S. domicile withhold tax in respect of the partnership shares of non-U.S. partners. Furthermore, in distinguishing between U.S. and non-U.S. partners, the requirement to withhold on the non-U.S. but not the U.S. partner's share is not discriminatory taxation, but, like other withholding on nonresident aliens, is merely a reasonable method for the collection of tax from persons who are not continually present in the United States, and as to whom it otherwise may be difficult for the United States to enforce its tax jurisdiction. If tax has been over-withheld, the partner can, as in other cases of over-withholding, file for a refund.

Paragraph 2 also provides that, notwithstanding the provisions of that paragraph, Sri Lanka retains the right to impose a tax on a permanent establishment of a U.S. enterprise under subsection 1(b) of Section 34 of Inland Revenue Act, No. 28 of 1979, as amended. However, the tax so imposed is limited to 15 percent of remittances, as defined in such section.

Paragraph 3

Paragraph 3 prohibits discrimination in the allowance of deductions. When a resident or enterprise of a Contracting State pays interest, royalties or other disbursements to a resident of the other Contracting State, the first-mentioned Contracting State must allow a deduction for those payments in computing the taxable profits of the resident or enterprise as if the payment had been made under the same conditions to a resident of the first-mentioned Contracting State. Paragraph 3, however, does not require a Contracting State to give non-residents more favorable treatment than it gives its own residents. Consequently, a Contracting State does not have to allow non-residents a deduction for items that are not deductible under its domestic law (for example, expenses of a capital nature).

The term "other disbursements" is understood to include a reasonable allocation of executive and general administrative expenses, research and development expenses and other expenses incurred for the benefit of a group of related persons that includes the person incurring the expense.

The opening part of the paragraph lists provisions of the Convention where the protection it gives for deductions does not apply. These are concerned with transactions involving potential abuse, where it is appropriate for the Contracting State to continue to apply their anti-avoidance safeguards. The paragraph carves out from its coverage the special relationship paragraphs at paragraph 1 of Article 9 (Associated Enterprises), paragraph 7 of Article 11 (Interest) or paragraph 7 of Article 12 (Royalties) because all of these provisions permit the denial of deductions in certain circumstances in respect of transactions between related persons. Neither State is forced to apply the non-discrimination principle in such cases. This exception with respect to paragraph 7 of Article 11 would include the denial or deferral of certain interest deductions under Code section 163(j).

Paragraph 3 also provides that any debts of a resident or enterprise of a Contracting State to a resident of the other Contracting State are deductible in the first-mentioned Contracting State for computing the capital tax of the enterprise under the same conditions as if the debt had been contracted to a resident of the first-mentioned Contracting State. Even though, for general purposes, the Convention covers only income taxes, under paragraph 6 of this Article, the nondiscrimination provisions apply to all taxes levied in both Contracting States, at all levels of government.

Paragraph 4

Paragraph 4 requires that a Contracting State not impose more burdensome taxation or connected requirements on an enterprise of that State that is wholly or partly owned or controlled, directly or indirectly, by one or more residents of the other Contracting State than the taxation or connected requirements that it imposes on other similar enterprises of that first-mentioned Contracting State. For this purpose it is understood that "similar" refers to similar activities or ownership of the enterprise.

This rule, like all non-discrimination provisions, does not prohibit differing treatment of entities that are in differing circumstances. Rather, a protected enterprise is only required to be treated in the same manner as other enterprises that, from the point of view of the application of the tax law, are in substantially similar circumstances both in law and in fact. The taxation of a distributing corporation under section 367(e) on an applicable distribution to foreign shareholders does not violate paragraph 4 of the Article because a foreign-owned corporation is not similar to a domestically-owned corporation that is accorded nonrecognition treatment under sections 337 and 355.

For the reasons given above in connection with the discussion of paragraph 2 of the Article, it is also understood that the provision in section 1446 of the Code for withholding of tax on non-U.S. partners does not violate paragraph 4 of the Article.

It is further understood that the ineligibility of a U.S. corporation with nonresident alien shareholders to make an election to be an "S" corporation does not violate paragraph 4 of the Article. If a corporation elects to be an S corporation (requiring 75 or fewer shareholders), it is generally not subject to income tax and the shareholders take into account their pro rata shares of the corporation's items of income, loss, deduction or credit. (The purpose of the provision is to allow an individual or small group of individuals to conduct business in corporate form while paying taxes at individual rates as if the business were conducted directly.) A nonresident alien does not pay U.S. tax on a net basis, and, thus, does not generally take into account items of loss, deduction or credit. Thus, the S corporation provisions do not exclude corporations with nonresident alien shareholders because such shareholders are foreign, but only because they are not net-basis taxpayers. Similarly, the provisions exclude corporations with other types of shareholders where the purpose of the provisions cannot be fulfilled or their mechanics implemented. For example, corporations with corporate shareholders are excluded because the purpose of the provision to permit individuals to conduct a business in corporate form at individual tax rates would not be furthered by their inclusion.

Paragraph 5

Paragraph 5 of the Article confirms that no provision of the Article will prevent either Contracting State from imposing the branch tax described in Article 12A (Branch Tax).

Paragraph 6

As noted above, notwithstanding the specification of taxes covered by the Convention in Article 2 (Taxes Covered) for general purposes, for purposes of providing non-discrimination protection this Article applies, in relation to the United States, to taxes of every kind imposed at a national level. In relation to Sri Lanka, the Article applies to all taxes administered by the Commissioner-General of Inland Revenue. Customs duties are not considered to be taxes for this purpose.

Relation to Other Articles

The saving clause of paragraph 3 of Article 1 (Personal Scope) does not apply to this Article, by virtue of the exceptions in paragraph 4(a) of Article 1. Thus, for example, a U.S. citizen who is a resident of the other Contracting State may claim benefits in the United States under this Article.

Nationals of a Contracting State may claim the benefits of paragraph 1 regardless of whether they are entitled to benefits under Article 23 (Limitation on Benefits), because that paragraph applies to nationals and not residents. They may not claim the benefits of the other paragraphs of this Article with respect to an item of income unless they are generally entitled to treaty benefits with respect to that income under a provision of Article 23.

Article 26 (Mutual Agreement Procedure)

This Article provides the mechanism for taxpayers to bring to the attention of the competent authorities of the Contracting States issues and problems that may arise under the Convention. This Article also provides a mechanism for cooperation between the competent authorities of the Contracting States to resolve disputes and clarify issues that may arise under the Convention and to resolve cases of double taxation not provided for in the Convention. The competent authorities of the two Contracting States are identified in subparagraph (i) of paragraph 1 of Article 3 (General Definitions).

Paragraph 1

This paragraph provides that where a person considers that the actions of one or both Contracting States will result in taxation that is not in accordance with the Convention he may present his case to the competent authority of the Contracting State of which he is a resident or national.

Although the typical cases brought under this paragraph will involve economic double taxation arising from transfer pricing adjustments, the scope of this paragraph is not limited to such cases. For example, if the United States treats income derived by a company resident in Sri Lanka as attributable to a permanent establishment in the United States, and the Sri Lankan resident believes that the income is not attributable to a permanent establishment, or that no permanent establishment exists, the Sri Lankan company may bring a complaint under paragraph 1 to the competent authority of Sri Lanka.

It is not necessary for a person bringing a complaint first to have exhausted the remedies provided under the national laws of the Contracting States before presenting a case to the competent authorities, nor does the fact that the statute of limitations may have passed for seeking a refund preclude bringing a case to the competent authority. Like the U.S. Model, no time limit is provided within which a case must be brought.

Paragraph 2

This paragraph instructs the competent authorities in dealing with cases brought by taxpayers under paragraph 1. Paragraph 2 provides that if the competent authority of the Contracting State to which the case is presented judges the case to have merit, and cannot reach a unilateral solution, it shall seek an agreement with the competent authority of the other Contracting State, pursuant to which taxation not in accordance with the Convention will be avoided.

Any agreement is to be implemented even if such implementation otherwise would be barred by the statute of limitations or by some other procedural limitation, such as a closing agreement. Paragraph 2, however, does not prevent the application of domestic-law procedural limitations that give effect to the agreement (*e.g.*, a domestic law requirement that the taxpayer file a return reflecting the agreement within one year of the agreement).

Where a taxpayer has entered a closing agreement (or other written settlement) with the United States prior to bringing a case to the competent authorities, the U.S. competent authority will endeavor only to obtain a correlative adjustment from Sri Lanka. *See* Rev. Proc. 2002-52, 2002-31 I.R.B. 242, § 7.04. Because, as specified in paragraph 2 of Article 1 (Personal Scope), the Convention cannot operate to increase a taxpayer's liability, temporal or other procedural limitations can be overridden only for the purpose of making refunds and not to impose additional tax.

Paragraph 3

Paragraph 3 authorizes the competent authorities to resolve difficulties or doubts that may arise as to the application or interpretation of the Convention. The paragraph includes a non-exhaustive list of examples of the kinds of matters about which the competent authorities may reach agreement. This list is purely illustrative; it does not grant any authority that is not implicitly present as a result of the introductory sentence of paragraph 3.

The competent authorities may, for example, agree to the same attribution of income, deductions, credits or allowances between an enterprise in one Contracting State and its permanent establishment in the other (subparagraph (a)) or between related persons (subparagraph (b)). These allocations are to be made in accordance with the arm's length principle underlying Article 7 (Business Profits) and Article 9 (Associated Enterprises). Agreements reached under these subparagraphs may include agreement on a methodology for determining an appropriate transfer price, common treatment of a taxpayer's cost sharing arrangement, or upon an acceptable range of results under that methodology.

As indicated in subparagraphs (c), (d), (e) and (g), the competent authorities also may agree to settle a variety of conflicting applications of the Convention. They may agree to characterize particular items of income in the same way (subparagraph (c)), to apply the same source rules to particular items of income (subparagraph (d)), and to adopt a common meaning of a term (subparagraph (e)). They also may agree as to the application of the provisions of domestic law regarding penalties, fines and interest in a manner consistent with the purposes of the Convention (subparagraph (g)).

Subparagraph (f) authorizes the competent authorities to increase any dollar amounts (but not percentages) referred to in the Convention to reflect economic and monetary developments. The rule under subparagraph (f) is intended to operate as follows: if, for example, after the Convention has been in force for some time, inflation rates have been such as to make the $6,000 exemption threshold for entertainers unrealistically low in terms of the original objectives intended in setting the threshold, the competent authorities may agree to a higher threshold without the need for formal amendment to the treaty and ratification by the Contracting States. This authority can be exercised, however, only to the extent necessary to restore those original objectives. Because of paragraph 2 of Article 1 (Personal Scope), it is clear that this provision can be applied only to the benefit of taxpayers, i.e., only to increase thresholds, not to reduce them.

Since the list under paragraph 3 is not exhaustive, the competent authorities may reach agreement on issues not enumerated in paragraph 3 if necessary to avoid double taxation. For example, the competent authorities may seek agreement on a uniform set of standards for the use of exchange rates, or agree on consistent timing of gain recognition with respect to a transaction to the extent necessary to avoid double taxation. Agreements reached under paragraph 3 need not conform to the internal law provisions of either Contracting State.

Finally, paragraph 3 authorizes the competent authorities to consult for the purpose of eliminating double taxation in cases not provided for in the Convention and to resolve any difficulties or doubts arising as to the interpretation or application of the Convention. This provision is intended to permit the competent authorities to implement the treaty in particular cases in a manner that is consistent with its expressed general purposes. It permits the competent authorities to deal with cases that are within the spirit of the provisions but that are not specifically covered. An example of such a case might be double taxation arising from a transfer pricing adjustment between two permanent establishments of a third-country resident, one in the United States and one in Sri Lanka. Since no resident of a Contracting State is involved in the case, the Convention does not apply, but the competent authorities nevertheless may use the authority of the Convention to prevent the double taxation.

Paragraph 4

Paragraph 4 provides that the competent authorities may communicate with each other for the purpose of reaching an agreement. This makes clear that the competent authorities of the two Contracting States may communicate without going through diplomatic channels. Such communication may be in various forms, including, where appropriate, through face-to-face meetings of representatives of the competent authorities.

Treaty effective dates and termination in relation to competent authority dispute resolution

A case may be raised by a taxpayer under a treaty with respect to a year for which a treaty was in force after the treaty has been terminated. In such a case the ability of the competent authorities to act is limited. They may not exchange confidential information, nor may they reach a solution that varies from that specified in their respective domestic laws.

A case also may be brought to a competent authority under a treaty that is in force, but with respect to a year prior to the entry into force of the treaty. The scope of the competent authorities to address such a case is not constrained by the fact that the treaty was not in force when the transactions at issue occurred, and the competent authorities have available to them the full range of remedies afforded under this Article.

Triangular competent authority solutions

International tax cases may involve more than two taxing jurisdictions (*e.g.*, transactions among a parent corporation resident in country A and its subsidiaries resident in countries B and C). As long as there is a complete network of treaties among the three countries, it should be possible, under the full combination of bilateral authorities, for the competent authorities of the three States to work together on a three-sided solution. Although country A may not be able to give information received under Article 27 (Exchange of Information) from country B to the authorities of country C, if the competent authorities of the three countries are working together, it should not be a problem for them to arrange for the authorities of country B to give the necessary information directly to the tax authorities of country C, as well as to those of country A. Each bilateral part of the trilateral solution must, of course, not exceed the scope of the authority of the competent authorities under the relevant bilateral treaty.

Relation to Other Articles

This Article is not subject to the saving clause of paragraph 3 of Article 1 (Personal Scope) by virtue of the exceptions in paragraph 4(a) of that Article. Thus, rules, definitions, procedures, etc. that are agreed upon by the competent authorities under this Article may be applied by the United States with respect to its citizens and residents even if they differ from the comparable Code provisions. Similarly, as indicated above, U.S. law may be overridden to provide refunds of tax to a U.S. citizen or resident under this Article.

A person may seek relief under Article 26 regardless of whether he is generally entitled to benefits under Article 23 (Limitation on Benefits). As in all other cases, the competent authority is vested with the discretion to decide whether the claim for relief is justified.

Article 27 (Exchange of Information and Administrative Assistance)

Paragraph 1

This Article provides for the exchange of information between the competent authorities of the Contracting States. The information to be exchanged is that which is relevant for carrying out the provisions of the Convention or the domestic laws of the United States or Sri Lanka concerning the taxes covered by the Convention. Like the OECD Model and earlier U.S. Models, but unlike the most recent U.S. Model, paragraph 1 refers to information that is "necessary" for carrying out the provisions of the Convention. This term consistently has been interpreted as being equivalent to "relevant," as used in the most recent U.S. Model, and does not require a requesting State to demonstrate that it would be prevented from enforcing its tax laws unless it obtained a particular item of information.

The taxes covered by the Convention for purposes of this Article constitute a broader category of taxes than those referred to in Article 2 (Taxes Covered). As provided in paragraph 6, for purposes of exchange of information, covered taxes include taxes of every kind imposed at the national level by the United States, and to all taxes administered by the Commissioner-General of Inland Revenue of Sri Lanka.

Exchange of information with respect to each State's domestic law is authorized insofar as the taxation under those domestic laws is not contrary to the Convention. Thus, for example, information may be exchanged with respect to a covered tax, even if the transaction to which the information relates is a purely domestic transaction in the requesting State and, therefore, the exchange is not made for the purpose of carrying out the Convention. An example of such a case is provided in the OECD Commentary: A company resident in the United States and a company resident in Sri Lanka transact business between themselves through a third-country resident company. Neither Contracting State has a treaty with the third State. In order to enforce their internal laws with respect to transactions of their residents with the third-country company (since there is no relevant treaty in force), the Contracting State may exchange information regarding the prices that their residents paid in their transactions with the third-country resident.

Paragraph 1 clarifies that information exchange is not restricted by Article 1 (Personal Scope). Accordingly, information may be requested and provided under this Article with respect to persons who are not residents of either Contracting State. For example, if a third-country resident has a permanent establishment in Sri Lanka which engages in transactions with a U.S. enterprise, the United States could request information with respect to that permanent establishment, even though the third-country resident is not a resident of either Contracting State. Similarly, if a third-country resident maintains a bank account in Sri Lanka, and the Internal Revenue Service has reason to believe that funds in that account should have been reported for U.S. tax purposes but have not been so reported, information can be requested from Sri Lanka with respect to that person's account, even though that person is not the taxpayer under examination.

Paragraph 1 also provides assurances that any information exchanged will be treated as secret, subject to the same disclosure constraints as information obtained under the laws of the requesting State. Information received may be disclosed only to persons, including courts and administrative bodies, involved in the assessment, collection, or administration of, the enforcement or prosecution in respect of, or the determination of the appeals in relation to, the taxes covered by the Convention. The information must be used by these persons in connection with these designated functions. Information received may be disclosed in public court proceedings or in judicial decisions.

The Article authorizes the competent authorities to exchange information on a routine basis, on request in relation to a specific case, or spontaneously. It is contemplated that the Contracting States will utilize this authority to engage in all of these forms of information exchange, as appropriate.

Paragraph 2

Paragraph 2 provides that the obligations undertaken in paragraph 1 to exchange information do not require a Contracting State to carry out administrative measures that are at variance with the laws or administrative practice of either State. Nor is a Contracting State required to supply information not obtainable under the laws or administrative practice of either State, or to disclose trade secrets or other information, the disclosure of which would be contrary to public policy. Thus, a requesting State may be denied information from the other State if the information would be obtained pursuant to procedures or measures that are broader than those available in the requesting State. However, each Contracting State has confirmed in the Notes its ability to obtain and exchange certain information under Article 27. The information that may be exchanged includes information held by financial institutions, nominees or persons acting in an agency or fiduciary capacity (not including information that would reveal confidential communications between a client and an attorney, where the client seeks legal advice). In the case of the United States, the scope of the privilege for such confidential communications is co-extensive with the attorney-client privilege under U.S. law. The Contracting States may also obtain and exchange information relating to the ownership of legal persons.

While paragraph 2 states conditions under which a Contracting State is not obligated to comply with a request from the other Contracting State for information, the requested State is not precluded from providing such information, and may, at its discretion, do so subject to the limitations of its internal law.

Paragraph 3

Paragraph 3 provides that when information is requested by a Contracting State in accordance with this Article, the other Contracting State is obligated to obtain the requested information as if the tax in question were the tax of the requested State, even if that State has no direct tax interest in the information requested.

Paragraph 3 further provides that the requesting State may specify the form in which such information is to be provided (*e.g.,* depositions of witnesses and authenticated copies of original documents) so that the information can be usable in the judicial proceedings of the requesting State. The requested State should, if possible, provide the information in the form requested to the same extent that it can obtain information in that form under its own laws and administrative practices with respect to its own taxes.
Paragraph 4

Paragraph 4 provides for assistance in collection of taxes to the extent necessary to ensure that treaty benefits are enjoyed only by persons entitled to those benefits under the terms of the Convention. Under paragraph 4, a Contracting State will endeavor to collect on behalf of the other State only those amounts necessary to ensure that any exemption or reduced rate of tax at source granted under the Convention by that other State is not enjoyed by persons not entitled to those benefits. For example, if the payer of a U.S.-source portfolio dividend receives a Form W-8BEN or other appropriate documentation from the payee, the withholding agent is permitted to withhold at the portfolio dividend rate of 15 percent. If, however, the addressee is merely acting as a nominee on behalf of a third-country resident, paragraph 4 would obligate Sri Lanka to take collection action against the person for the difference in applicable withholding rates in response to a specific request from the U.S. competent authority.

Paragraph 5

Paragraph 5 makes clear that the Contracting State asked to collect the tax pursuant to paragraph 4 is not obligated, in the process of providing such assistance, to carry out administrative measures that are different from those used in the collection of its own taxes, or that would be contrary to its sovereignty, security or public policy.

Paragraph 6

As noted above in the discussion of paragraph 1, the exchange of information provisions of the Convention apply to taxes of every kind imposed by the at the national level by the United States, and to all taxes administered by the Commissioner-General of Inland Revenue of Sri Lanka. The U.S. competent authority may, therefore, request information for purposes of, for example, estate and gift taxes or federal excise taxes.

Treaty effective dates and termination in relation to exchange of information

Once the Convention is in force, the competent authority may seek information under the Convention with respect to a year prior to the entry into force of the Convention. Even though the Convention was not in effect during the years in which the transaction at issue occurred, the exchange of information provisions of the Convention apply. In that case, the competent authorities have available to them the full range of information exchange provisions afforded under this Article.

A tax administration may also seek information with respect to a year for which a treaty was in force after the treaty has been terminated. In such a case the ability of the other tax administration to act is limited. The treaty no longer provides authority for the tax administrations to exchange confidential information. They may only exchange information pursuant to domestic law.

Article 28 (Diplomatic Agents and Consular Officers)

This Article confirms that any fiscal privileges to which diplomatic or consular officials are entitled under general provisions of international law or under special agreements will apply notwithstanding any provisions to the contrary in the Convention. The agreements referred to include any bilateral agreements, such as consular conventions, that affect the taxation of diplomats and consular officials and any multilateral agreements dealing with these issues, such as the Vienna Convention on Diplomatic Relations and the Vienna Convention on Consular Relations. The U.S. generally adheres to the latter because its terms are consistent with customary international law.

The Article does not independently provide any benefits to diplomatic agents and consular officers. Article 20 (Government Service) does so, as do Code section 893 and a number of bilateral and multilateral agreements. In the event that there is a conflict between the Convention and international law or such other treaties, under which the diplomatic agent or consular official is entitled to greater benefits under the latter, the latter laws or agreements shall have precedence. Conversely, if the tax treaty confers a greater benefit than another agreement, the affected person could claim the benefit of the tax treaty.

Pursuant to subparagraph 4(b) of Article 1, the saving clause of paragraph 3 of Article 1 (Personal Scope) does not apply to override any benefits of this Article available to an individual who is neither a citizen of the United States nor has immigrant status there.

Article 29 (Entry into Force)

This Article contains the rules for bringing the Convention into force and giving effect to its provisions.

Paragraph 1

Paragraph 1 provides for the ratification of the Convention by both Contracting States according to their constitutional and statutory requirements. Instruments of ratification shall be exchanged as soon as possible.

The Protocol amending the Convention, signed September 20, 2002, provides that the Protocol shall also be subject to ratification in accordance with the applicable procedures of each Contracting State and that instruments of ratification shall be exchanged as soon as possible.

In the United States, the process leading to ratification and entry into force is as follows: once a treaty has been signed by authorized representatives of the two Contracting States, the Department of State sends the treaty to the President who formally transmits it to the Senate for its advice and consent to ratification, which requires approval by two-thirds of the Senators present and voting. Prior to this vote, however, it generally has been the practice for the Senate Committee on Foreign Relations to hold hearings on the treaty and make a recommendation regarding its approval to the full Senate. Both Government and private sector witnesses may testify at these hearings. After receiving the advice and consent of the Senate to ratification, the treaty is returned to the President for his signature on the ratification document. The President's signature on the document completes the process in the United States.

Paragraph 2

Paragraph 2 provides that the Convention will enter into force upon exchange of instruments of ratification. The date on which a treaty enters into force is not necessarily the date on which its provisions take effect. Paragraph 2, therefore, also contains rules that determine when the provisions of the treaty will have effect.

Under paragraph 2(a), the Convention will have effect with respect to taxes withheld at source (principally dividends, interest and royalties) for amounts paid or credited on or after the first day of the second month following the date on which the Convention enters into force. For example, if instruments of ratification are exchanged on April 25 of a given year, the withholding rates specified in paragraph 2 of Article 10 (Dividends) would be applicable to any dividends paid or credited on or after June 1 of that year. This rule allows the benefits of the withholding reductions to be put into effect quickly, while allowing sufficient time for withholding agents to be informed about the change in withholding rates. If for some reason a withholding agent withholds at a higher rate than that provided by the Convention (perhaps because it was not able to re-program its computers before the payment is made), a beneficial owner of the income that is a resident of Sri Lanka may make a claim for refund pursuant to section 1464 of the Code.

With respect to all other taxes (including the branch profits tax), paragraph 2(b) specifies that the Convention will have effect for any taxable year or assessment period beginning on or after January 1 of the year in which the Convention enters into force.

As discussed under Articles 26 (Mutual Agreement Procedure) and 27 (Exchange of Information), the powers afforded the competent authority under these articles apply retroactively to taxable periods preceding entry into force.

Article 30 (Termination)

The Convention is to remain in effect indefinitely, unless terminated by one of the Contracting States in accordance with the provisions of Article 30. The Convention may be terminated at any time after 5 years from the date on which the Convention enters into force. A Contracting State seeking to terminate the Convention must give at least six months' notice through diplomatic channels.

If notice of termination is given, the provisions of the Convention with respect to withholding at source will cease to have effect for payments made or credited on or after January 1 next following the expiration of the six month notification period. With respect to other taxes, the Convention will cease to have effect with respect to income of taxable years beginning on or after January 1 next following the expiration of the six month notification period.

Article 30 relates only to unilateral termination of the Convention by a Contracting State. Nothing in that Article should be construed as preventing the Contracting States from concluding a new bilateral agreement, subject to ratification, that supersedes, amends or terminates provisions of the Convention without the six-month notification period.

Customary international law observed by the United States and other countries, as reflected in the Vienna Convention on Treaties, allows termination by one Contracting State at any time in the event of a "material breach" of the agreement by the other Contracting State.

Protocol

A Protocol accompanies and forms part of the Convention. The provisions of Articles I through XIX of the Protocol are discussed in connection with the relevant Articles of the Convention.